SATURATE

Endorsements

We have seen the devil's best move! Now get ready to see God's *biggest* and best move in history. Jessi Green, a proven revivalist, prophetically describes this outpouring and its timing to a Christian world that is *unprepared!* The *best* is yet to come!

—**Sid Roth**
TV Host, *It's Supernatural!*

Jessi Green's book, *Saturate,* will truly inspire you to go all out for Jesus! She shares not only from biblical understanding but from authentic experience. If you are desiring to live "all in," this is your read!

—**Patricia King**
Author, Minister, Media Host and Producer
www.patriciaking.com

Right before the turn of the millennium, God gave me a significant dream. In this dream was a map of North America, where I saw "red dots" appear on the map, this was followed by a "wind," that caused the smoldering red dots to burn the map away. As this map was burned off, underneath was the most beautiful golden grain that I had ever seen. I immediately was given the understanding that God has set up revival hot spots across North America, in which a wind of the Spirit would blow, a spiritual igniting would take place, and the result would be a harvest like we have never seen.

Jessi Green's new book, *Saturate,* is giving us a both a trumpet blast and blueprints for this unusual move that God is sending to gather in an end-time harvest that will stagger the nations. But first, God is dealing with His bride to rise up to the designation she was given in the heart of the Father from eons past. We will truly witness Heaven on display in an unprecedented fashion.

Jessi is truly an authentic prophetic and poignant voice whom God has raised up in this hour. As I read this manuscript, my heart burned (like the map I was shown in the heavenly vision), and I felt stirred again to see what Jessi writes about come to pass. This book is sure to do the same to you!

—Sean Smith
Author of *I Am Your Sign* and *Prophetic Evangelism*
Podcase Co-Host of *Keep It 100 w/ Sean and Christa Smith*
www.seanandchristasmith.com

In her newest book, *Saturate*, Jessi Green helps us understand the heart behind revival and shares prophetic insight for the days ahead. I consider Parker and Jessi Green family to me and forerunners for multigenerational revival. I have personally witnessed their hunger and humility to continue learning, risking, and growing. They invite, empower, and propel others to join them in awakening the bride of Christ to the urgency of the hour. Jessi writes with both clarity and anointing, delivering a passionate, compelling message for each of us to pursue revival as a lifestyle. It's time to step in! *Saturate* will light a fire in your soul and give you the tools to step into a life of miracles in Jesus.

—Reverend Joanne Moody
Agape Freedom Fighters
Agape Apostolic Equipping and Training Center
LIFE School

Early in 2022, I was attending a small event with business and ministry leaders from across the nation. One of the topics for discussion was "Revival" and Jessi shared her passion and heart to see a nation transformed. It is there where I became acquainted with Jessi and connected to her ministry, "Saturate." Jessi is one of the most real and authentic voices in our generation, pioneering true revival. I believe that when people read her new book, *Saturate*, a renewed hunger will be provoked in every reader. Jesus is real, and I believe our generation is seeing that. I have a dream to see Gen Z suicide-free—and it will take revival to save those who are hurting.

—Jacob Coyne
Director, Stay Here
"Gen Z Will Be Suicide-Free"
www.stayhere.live

When you reach a saturation point, you enter a time when no more can be absorbed and anything added could create an overflow. When most Christians approach saturation, they misinterpret it as satisfaction and walk away from the overflow God has for them, thinking they are full and have need of nothing (Revelation 3:17). Revivals often spoil on the vine for this very reason. This book is a fail-safe against this deadly satisfaction. *Saturate* will not only awaken within you a hunger for the excessive outpouring of the Spirit, but it will provide a roadmap for you to go beyond satisfaction and on into prophetic fulfillment. You *will* see revival!

In her own unfiltered style, Jessi Green boldly shares the vision God has for His Church and how we cannot only survive but thrive in the shaking that's coming. Get ready to have your eyes opened to what God is doing on earth today and be equipped to take part in the end-time awakening. Powerful and at times provocative, this book is a wake-up call that I pray every believer will read and heed!

—**Alan DiDio**
Encounter Today

We are in the most historic time of awakening in the history of Christianity. The apostle Paul shares in Romans 13:11 (TPT), *"To live like this is all the more urgent, for time is running out and you know it is a strategic hour in human history. It is time for us to wake up!"* Friends, we are in this strategic hour, an era, when there is a rousing out of slumber, a waking up. There is a passion and fire stirring within believers, the Church, and the lost world. Holy Spirit is awakening a revival transformational move. It is not Church as usual for those who are wanting the abundant more of who He is and the baptism of fire into a holy surrender and burning revival promise available to each of us as our Kingdom of Heaven inheritance. If you are hungry for the truth, longing to be stirred to awakening and challenged to go all in for the Holy Spirit fires of revival, *Saturate: An Invitation to Go All In for Revival* is a must read for you. Thank you, Jessi, for this now word and message. And for your voice of awakening that is resounding with the message of revival fires for this era.

—**Rebecca Greenwood**
Cofounder, Christian Harvest International
Strategic Prayer Apostolic Network

My beautiful friend Jessi Green has penned deep, prophetic wisdom and insight from the heart of God in her latest book, *Saturate*. As Jessi shares her vision of each of the seven waves and what it means for the harvest, there is a deep and loud clarion call resounding, "Will you be all in for Jesus?" and "Will you arise as part of the revival remnant?" in this hour. This incredible book will not only arm you with revelation and insight for the days to come, but also position you in *His* ways for this new era. *Saturate* will help you understand the weight of the hour in which we are living and ignite a fire in you to see the birthing of revival and the harvest on earth. I cannot recommend this book highly enough for this new era.

—Lana Vawser
Author

Around 50 years ago, the world was in terrible turmoil with wars, racial conflict, political polarization, and a global pandemic. God responded by sending a powerful revival that resulted in the Jesus People Movement that drew us back from the edge of calamity. At this moment in history, global turmoil is even greater and the hope for human solutions is quickly fading. Our only hope is a new wave of revival.

In her latest book, Jessi Green makes a brilliant case for the urgent need of revival in our generation. She combines her amazing personal story with powerful testimonies of revival breaking out in key regions across the nation. Jessi and Parker Green have been instrumental in hosting outpourings of the Holy Spirit that have brought salvation, healing, and freedom to thousands. In addition, she lays down a roadmap for how we can partner with God for the next Great Awakening. *Saturate* will lay hold of your heart, strip away all excuses, and empower you to become the revivalist God created you to be. This book is required reading "for such a time as this!"

—**Michael Brodeur**
Director of LeadersAlliance.org
Co-author, *Revival Culture: Prepare for the Next Great Awakening!*

Raise your hand if you have waited your whole life to see the miracles you grew up reading about. *Saturate* is the blueprint for how we can be awakened and to accept the invitation to show up. You will not be able to put this book down, and when you do, you will know that today, right now, is your time to answer, "Here I am. Send me." This is it. This is the move your life, passions, and gifts have been aching for! This is the moment you have always asked the Lord to see—and now you get to be part of it.

—Jeanne Oliver
Artist and Author
jeanneoliver.com

Saturate is a brave, urgent, and needed book for this hour. It is not to be picked up and read flippantly, but with intentionality. Jessi is not one to pull punches, but also holds a tension throughout this book of speaking the *truth in love* that is hard to find in this day and age. I found myself weeping, laughing, and pausing to dig deep and ask myself where I needed to repent and live differently. This book will mark you if you let it; it will draw you deeper, causing you to go "all in" for Jesus.

—Andi Andrew
Author and Speaker

In classic "Jessi" fashion, *Saturate* is raw, honest, and transparent. This book functions as an urgent warning to the Body of Christ, as well as a field manual for revival. Jessi Green addresses the many challenges we face within the Church; however, she also provides legitimate and practical solutions. The results of trial by fire. I urge you, whether you feel lost, are lacking purpose, or have been earnestly praying for revival in your city or state, let this book bring the necessary conviction and change into your life. Take these words to heart and burn bright!

—Jeff Tharp
Host of *ElijahFire*

Be warned, reading this book will leave a lasting effect on your life! *Saturate* is more than just another book, it's a heart adjustment, a temperature check, and call to action for revival. I read this with equal measure of tears and a deep burning in my bones for more. While Jessi shares prophetic insight for this crucial season of harvest, she equally shares practical, revival-road-tested wisdom that we've watched work.

It's our great honor to call Jessi and Parker Green our friends, and an even greater honor to have "gone to war" for the Gospel with them! Their radical obedience and raw faith has left a lasting effect on our lives and family.

We wholeheartedly recommend not only this book to you, but the heart of its author, as one who is wrecked for the ordinary, and known in heaven and hell as a giant in the land. We know as you read *Saturate*, you'll be provoked to pursue revival and radically compelled to give Jesus your "costly yes" for eternity's sake.

—Ben and Jodie Hughes
Pour It Out Ministries
www.pouritout.org
Revivalists, Media Missionaries
Authors, *When God Breaks In, The King's Decree, The King's Prophetic Voice*

DESTINY IMAGE BOOKS BY JESSI GREEN

Wildfires:
A Field Guide to Supernatural Revival

SATURATE

LEAVING *Behind* *S*TATUS QUO RELIGION FOR A FAITH THAT REALLY *W*ORKS

JESSI GREEN

DESTINY IMAGE® PUBLISHERS, INC.
P.O. Box 310, Shippensburg, PA 17257-0310
"Promoting Inspired Lives."

This book and all other Destiny Image and Destiny Image Fiction books are available at Christian bookstores and distributors worldwide.

For more information on foreign distributors, call 717-532-3040.

Reach us on the Internet: www.destinyimage.com.

ISBN 13 TP: 978-0-7684-6290-6

ISBN 13 eBook: 978-0-7684-6291-3

ISBN 13 HC: 978-0-7684-6293-7

ISBN 13 LP: 978-0-7684-6292-0

For Worldwide Distribution, Printed in the U.S.A.

1 2 3 4 5 6 7 8 / 27 26 25 24 23

Dedication

I dedicate this book to my sons, David and Ethan Green. My hope is that you read these words and remember what we sacrificed for. I pray protection and victory over both your lives, to see souls saved and hell pillaged. Always remember, our family is *all in* for revival, to see our nation saved and set free. We will sell all, give all, and lay down our lives to prepare a place for the Holy Spirit to come. I pray that you both will *always* know the real Jesus and that God will pursue you both hotly.

"Obedience Is Success" —Green Family Motto

Contents

*T*here are seven waves of awakening coming.
Each wave is a key to the billions-soul harvest.
We are in the midst of this—now.

Foreword

by Corey Russell

I'm convinced that the body of Christ and especially the charismatic section of it is in a pivotal moment in history. Those who have birthed past moves of God and those who have read the most on revival are in danger of having all the language of revival and understanding of it—while living so far from it. My fear is that we've become inoculated to the reality of it and have redefined and lowered the true definition of revival.

It was this burden that drove us last year to write *Reclaiming Revival* and I believe we need many voices rising up in these days calling us, provoking us, and challenging us to freshly sow our lives into the ground to see another great awakening touch our nation as well as the whole earth.

This is why I am beyond grateful for Jessi Green and her new book, *Saturate: An Invitation to Go All In for Revival*. I've followed Jessi and her husband, Parker, over the last few years and I've found that their abandonment to God is giving courage and vision to a generation to believe again for a true, historic outpouring of the Holy Spirit in our nation.

The prophet Hosea is crying out to this generation, "Break up your fallow ground, for it is time to seek the Lord till He comes and rains righteousness on you," and I can hear the prophet's cry in the pages of this book. God has woven the same prophetic cry through the life of Jessi for this generation, and you will quickly see the same power resting on her words. Jessi has gone all in for revival, and it's because of her surrender to the will of God, that authority rings through her call to us. I invite you to slowly and prayerfully read through this book.

I beg you to not merely consume one more book to put on your shelf and say, "I read that"—rather, I pray that you would let these words cut you, confront you, and call you to go *all in* for revival.

—**Corey Russell**
Author and Speaker
coreyrussell.org

Introduction

I have died a thousand deaths.

As I begin to write this book, I find myself again, hungry for more of God, desperate for Him to do something in us and through us that can save our nation. I believe that we are at a crossroad. While this book can be inspiring and equip anyone in any nation, I do write earnestly to my fellow American. I know that in doing so, I risk the chance of limiting my reach; however, my heart is bleeding with each vein a frayed wire, as I anguish over the condition of our culture and more importantly the state of the Church in the United States of America.

In my early years of ministry, I found myself drawn to the streets. Looking for those who were hidden away, tucked into the darkness of their own souls, seeking refuge from the torment that surrounded them. The hungry, the hurting, the broken. It was there where I saw God moving, and the Holy Spirit was drawing convicted felons, night-club promoters, and the poor in spirit into His Kingdom.

In 2017, over a Christmas holiday in Seattle, I found myself penning into my new journal, "You are no longer an evangelist. You are a revivalist."

I'll be honest, I am not one who yearned to be a revivalist, nor was I trained in a supernatural school—although I wish I was! In a way, I was commissioned by God, wrestling with the idea of if one could even be commissioned by God! Reading Paul's letter to the Galatians:

> But when he [God] who had set me apart before I was born, and who called me by his grace, was pleased to reveal his Son to me, in order that I might preach him among the Gentiles, I did not immediately consult with anyone.
>
> (Galatians 1:15-16 ESV)

Hidden away, searching online "What is a revivalist?" and praying for the Lord to train me and show me which way to go. To be commissioned by God, what an honor that needs to be stewarded by every believer.

We face a terrifying time in today's culture—as false humility pervades our ministries, and comparison has us praying, seeking, decreeing for a mantle that was never ours to begin with.

I write this book as an invitation to you. An invitation to settle in your spirit that you will stop faking it. That you will come to the end of yourself and discover what God Himself may commission you to do. That you will quit living one foot in the world, and one foot in the Kingdom, commanding that the Lord of Hosts serve you in your dreams and ambitions.

I pray that the spirit of false humility would come off you, and quickly! That you can hear from God, submit to your assignment, and without fear or wavering, know what and to whom you are called. I pray that you don't allow the enemy to lull you asleep, into a slumber of self-care and self-idolatry. That the cultural pressures of social justice would not bait you, hooking your cheek and stomping the life out of the last flickering embers of light in your ever-seeking soul.

What God is orchestrating right now is an international invitation *into more*. A full cultural transformation preceded by revival and being sustained through reformation and renaissance. If we do not lay down our plans and co-labor with the Creator of the universe, we will be subjected to the ramifications of a culture that is in rebellion. We must say "yes" to Him, over and over again.

GOD IS ORCHESTRATING RIGHT NOW AN INTERNATIONAL INVITATION INTO MORE.

Over the past two years, God has entrusted me to lead revival. I am not the only person catalyzing revival, of course not! However, He has given our family an opportunity to lead something that is unique and essential in the days ahead. I approach this subject with caution and honor for the pioneers who have paved the way in revival in our nation and will include key lessons I have learned from generals in the faith.

My first book, *Wildfires*, shares the gritty reality of leading revival and how to be ignited with the Spirit of God. I wrote this book, *Saturate*, with great urgency, as I witnessed across the nation how ill-equipped the saints are for the times we are living in. We need to take hold of what the new thing is that God is doing, and we need to prophetically see and shift our way of doing things to transform the culture to look more like the Kingdom of God.

Late September 2020, the Lord woke me up in the middle of the night. I saw a vision of giant waves rolling into the shores of California. As each wave crashed in, the waters covered the state and slowly rolled through the rest of the nation. As the wave drew back slowly, there was a pause before the next larger wave crashed in harder and more violently.

In an effort to engage as many people in this nation in this next move of God, I will break down to the best of my ability what I saw with each wave, as I have spent time in prayer and testing the word with other prophets. I will also share some of the brutal lessons I have had to learn while leading revival, so that you will not find yourself discouraged and beaten in the midst of so much opportunity and opposition.

I pray these words both stir up your faith, open your eyes to see, and draw you in deeper to know the love of Jesus and to believe that He wants revival more than we do. **I believe that we so rarely see revival historically, because we so rarely see a group of people who love Jesus more than themselves.** We have a nation of "Christians" who are not reborn from above.

But mark this: **There will be terrible times in the last days.** *People will be lovers of themselves, lovers of money, boastful, proud, abusive, disobedient to their parents, ungrateful, unholy, without love, unforgiving, slanderous, without self-control, brutal, not lovers of the good, treacherous, rash, conceited, lovers of pleasure rather than lovers of God—***having a form of godliness but denying its power. Have nothing to do with such people.*** *They are the kind who worm their way into homes and gain control over gullible women, who are loaded down with sins and are swayed by all kinds of evil desires,* **always learning but never able to come to a knowledge of the truth.**

(2 Timothy 3:1-10 NIV)

THE FUTURE OF THE UNITED STATES OF AMERICA DEPENDS ON HOW THE SAINTS RESPOND TO GOD'S PLAN.

Over and over again, I find myself coming to the end of myself. The end of my abilities and needing to rely fully on the Holy Spirit. Never before have I experienced the Scriptures truly coming to life, like they are right now. Each event that we host, I find myself dying once again to myself, picking up my cross and following Jesus. My time in prayer has now looked like times of abandon as I lay down plans, sell my belongings, and risk over and over in an effort to do what I believe the Holy Spirit is asking.

I pray that as you read this book, that you don't just do what I am doing. I pray that the Holy Spirit would speak to you personally and that you would obey Him. I pray that if God gives you a vision of a place, that you pay attention. I pray that generosity would overflow in you and through you as you become a vessel to exchange money for souls. This is not the hour to hold back. This is not the hour to wait for 1,000 confirmations. This is the hour to ascend, to lift up your eyes, to get higher and bring others with you.

Will you die to your way of living and give your life as a living and holy sacrifice?

Imagine the ripple of revival that could take place.

1

Genesis of Revival

Even now the axe is laid to the root of the trees. Every tree therefore that does not bear good fruit is cut down and thrown into the fire. "I baptize you with water for repentance, but he who is coming after me is mightier than I, whose sandals I am not worthy to carry. He will baptize you with the Holy Spirit and fire"

(Matthew 3:10-11 ESV).

The year 2016 was a pivotal year prophetically.

I know for our family, personally, it was a year of great transition and change. As I have met with other key leaders about this next great revival, many stories around the dinner table often begin with "In 2016..."

I dare say, this next great revival and/or awakening in America, began in 2016, but so few of us had eyes to see what the Lord was truly doing and preparing us for. For many of us, we felt a lot shifted spiritually on a national level. The year 2016 was when God asked our family to lay everything down in New York City to be part of the revival He was beginning in Orange County, California.

At this point, we had only heard a few things about the Jesus People Movement and didn't know anything about the revival history of California. Keep in mind, when God was inviting us to lay down everything, sell everything and move across the country, there were no signs of revival breaking out in California, in fact, quite the contrary.

TAKING THE GREAT COMMISSION SERIOUSLY

My husband, Parker, and I felt with great urgency that we needed to take the Great Commission seriously and prepare nets for discipleship. God spoke to Parker one early morning on our Manhattan rooftop about creating blueprints for an unstoppable Church. The Lord said to Parker, "How do you grow and build an unstoppable Church? What if tomorrow there was a terrorist attack or pandemic? What if you weren't allowed to meet anymore? How would the Church move forward?"

Parker then thought, *What if there were a church in every home? What if we stopped inviting people to not only come to gatherings—but also equip them to be full of the Holy Spirit and then send them out in real, working miracle power?*

A few months earlier in January 2016, my worship session at a conference was interrupted by an open vision of mass baptisms in Huntington Beach. I kept hearing the Lord say, "I'm drawing a line in the sand. During the next few years, you will know very clearly who is for Me or against Me."

I felt in my spirit that the days of being lukewarm were over for the Church. We needed to rise up. We need to know the Word *and* be filled with the Holy Spirit. As a nation, we traded God's presence for programs, and we needed to repent.

*W*E NEED TO KNOW THE WORD AND BE FILLED WITH THE HOLY SPIRIT.

Over the next few months, we spoke to our lead pastors about what God was speaking to us. With tears in their eyes, they said that they believed God was calling us to California and they needed to release us to go for the sake of souls. Reality began to set in, pregnant with our first baby and now making plans to move to a place where we knew no one. As the year progressed, we sold our things and began to pray and dream into the next season of our lives.

We transitioned the church campuses in Manhattan we were overseeing, and moved out of our luxury doorman apartment into a small back room in my in-laws' Brooklyn apartment. I cried and grieved—every dream that I had prayed into for our lives in New York City was being put to death. Leaving our family, our best friends, our full-time salaries—all to risk and try to follow the leading of the Holy Spirit. We didn't know what we were doing, and could not truly prepare for the victories and hardships that were ahead.

September 2016, we were packed up for our trek to California. Parker and I drove 18 hours from Brooklyn, New York, to Gainesville, Georgia, to speak at an Awakening Conference at Adventures in Missions. The conference was focused on stirring up faith in the hearts of former short-term millennial missionaries. During the drive down with our now 3-week-old firstborn—which I wouldn't advise for any future parents, ha!—we looked up potential rental apartments in Huntington Beach, California. With plans to move in the next month, after stepping down from our full-time pastoral positions, we were grieving the season we were leaving while being so completely agitated by the Holy Spirit's invitation to go all in, *in this new thing He was doing*.

At the four-day conference, the Lord told me that He was going to highlight the importance of baptisms. Up until this point, I had only baptized people during organized, quarterly church baptism services. As I prepared to preach that morning, I kept crying as I could feel the presence of God pressing me to risk with Him. I told our mentor, Clint, "I think God wants us to baptize people this afternoon, but we don't have any baptismals."

Clint spoke words that would catalyze my entire future. He said, **"Jessi, if the Lord is telling you to do something. You do it. We will figure it out."**

An hour later, some of the team put a brown tarp in the back of a large pickup truck and began to fill it with hose water. I felt like my nerves were being electrocuted. I had about five messages prepared to preach, but none of them felt quite right. I rocked my baby, David, under my arms, wiping sweat off my forehead as we sat on metal folding chairs under a wooden awning outside. I closed my eyes and prayed, "God, I need a word from You."

I started to cry as I could feel that this moment was shifting something. What, I had no idea.

I heard the Lord say, "I am drawing a line in the sand." I wept at the idea of people deciding *not* to choose God, choosing *not* to go all in and give Him everything. After worship, I stepped onto the stage and began to read a Psalm. I don't even remember which one, because it was such a quick prompting to open it and read it. I thought, *I'll read this Psalm and then get to my message.* Up until this point, I had only preached three-point, outlined sermons that were part of our church's sermon series.

"JESSI, IF THE LORD IS TELLING YOU TO DO SOMETHING. YOU DO IT. WE WILL FIGURE IT OUT."

A BIRTH PAIN OF REVIVAL

As I read the Psalm, I just couldn't stop crying. I choked as I read each word, looking like a fool up on the stage. I then knelt down and repented on behalf of every person who had participated in short-term missions with the organization and had slandered or gossiped about one another.

I cried out to God and people ran forward, crying out in repentance. I honestly can't explain what happened next, but looking back now I would say that it very much was a birth pain of revival.

I ended up preaching for only a few minutes after this "repentance cry fest" and said, "The dry season is a lie! You shall have rivers of living water! I walked over to the pickup truck filled with water, not looking back but praying over and over in the Spirit, hoping people were behind me. Over the next few hours, more than seventy-five people decided to get baptized in the back of a dirty pickup truck in a small town in the middle of Georgia. There is something significant about baptisms in this next move of God.

"HIS WORDS TO US ARE SPIRIT AND LIFE, TRANSFORMING US AND CHANGING US, EXPELLING THAT WHICH IS NATURAL AND BRINGING IN THAT WHICH IS DIVINE."

–Smith Wigglesworth

2

Secrets of the Kingdom

And he answered them, "To you it has been given to know the secrets of the kingdom of heaven, but to them it has not been given. For to the one who has, more will be given, and he will have an abundance, but from the one who has not, even what he has will be taken away. This is why I speak to them in parables, because seeing they do not see, and hearing they do not hear, nor do they understand. Indeed, in their case the prophecy of Isaiah is fulfilled that says: 'You will indeed hear but never understand, and you will indeed see but never perceive.' For this people's heart has grown dull, and with their ears they can barely hear, and their eyes they have closed, lest they should see with their eyes and hear with their ears and understand with their heart and turn, and I would heal them."

(Matthew 13:1-15 ESV)

Over the past six years, we have met with several churches and ministry leaders throughout the United States. I could not believe how many churches, with tears in their eyes, were at a total loss when it came to making disciples, especially followers of Jesus who would also, in fact, disciple others. When surveyed, most members in the congregations didn't know the Gospel and had never shared their faith with anyone in the last year. My husband, Parker, wrestled through the night in prayer and jotted down in his journal, "The saints need to be equipped." **I've found that the late night wrestles, the small phrases that the Holy Spirit deposits into us, are bread crumbs on a trail into our identity and purpose in Jesus.**

As many of you know, as I explain in great detail the journey in my book *Wildfires*, in 2019 the Lord gave me a word that would change everything for us and many others to come. The Lord said, "The harvest begins summer 2020, prepare the nets." As we prayed, planned, and prepared to do an evangelism training and conference during the US Open of Surfing—one of the largest events in Southern California—plans changed over and over again. We applied for permits, visited hotel venues, and smoked brisket in the backyard as we cast vision to whoever in Orange County would listen. Several pastors refused to meet for coffee, and I very much felt like the annoying persistent widow.

Without name recognition and a prominent ministry, I felt discouraged by the task at hand and would repeatedly question if I had heard from God at all. I believe that for many of us, in our journey of faith, this is when we quit. When the doors close and favor is found elsewhere, we begin to be like Eve in the garden, tempted by that same slithering snake. "Did God really say…?" This is the question that holds so many of us back from the promises that will only be realized by risky faith in partnership with the Holy Spirit.

As we continued to plan, January 2020, the Lord said, "I'm separating the wheat from the tares…." We believe that this is the first wave of revival, which we are currently experiencing and fully in. I wish I had started this book earlier, which is why I write with such great urgency. At this point, this first wave is not prophetic, this is just news that we see on a weekly basis. That winter, we never could have expected that a global pandemic would shut down many of the churches around the world from meeting. As many of us learned to bake bread, hoard toilet paper, and take up gardening while in quarantine, I kept seeking God, looking for an "out."

Events worldwide were now cancelled and it became a rebellious act to meet in a home with more than eight people. I was now 30 weeks pregnant with our third child, Summer, who was due to be born just eight weeks before our first "Saturate" gathering. Without a venue, and a spreadsheet full of rejections from speakers, we kept praying. Late one evening I heard the Lord whisper, "Jessi, I did not lie. The harvest begins this summer."

I'll admit, I wanted the harvest to come another time.

Fast-forward to the summer of 2020 when we had the opportunity to baptize thousands of people on the beaches of Southern California, as a remnant of sold-out believers were surfacing across the nation. My social media feed became flooded with reports of people just going for it, baptizing others in the streets and launching media ministries. I believe that God is bridging the gap between denominational and generational lines and cleaning house for the harvest. My book titled *Wildfires* breaks down what we saw, what we experienced, and what we learned during that time.

What may appear to be division is in fact, God uniting *His* Church, separating true followers of the Gospel from principalities that have been masquerading behind religious activity and a form a godliness but lacking power.

WHAT MAY APPEAR TO BE DIVISION IS IN FACT, GOD UNITING HIS CHURCH, SEPARATING TRUE FOLLOWERS OF THE GOSPEL FROM PRINCIPALITIES THAT HAVE BEEN MASQUERADING BEHIND RELIGIOUS ACTIVITY AND A FORM A GODLINESS BUT LACKING POWER.

SEVEN WAVES

After six weeks of hosting revival in Southern California, we felt the Lord leading us to "pause" and come into the "secret place" for further instruction. I grieved, wondering if this was the greatest thing we would ever experience in our Christianity and we were laying it down.

September 18, 2020, the Lord woke me up in the middle of the night. I saw a vision of giant waves rolling onto the shores of California. As each wave crashed in, the waters covered the state and slowly rolled through the rest of the nation. As the wave drew back slowly, there was a pause before the next larger wave crashed in harder and more violently.

The bride of Christ, is awakening to the love of Jesus and the power of the Holy Spirit as we re-prioritize the preaching of the Gospel and the Great Commission of making disciples who have unbroken fellowship with Jesus. As the Saints are being trained, equipped, and sent, we are starting to see the fruit of lives that are born again.

KEYS OF AWAKENING

The Seven Waves:

1. The First Wave – Wheat, Tares, and the Remnant

2. The Second Wave – Resurrection of the Unborn

3. The Third Wave – Prophetic Showdown

4. The Fourth Wave – National Repentance

5. The Fifth Wave – Cleaning House

6. The Sixth Wave – Exposure

7. The Seventh Wave – Pioneers and Frontiers

In the following chapters, I break down and explain what each wave represents, what we can learn, and how we can respond to be on our front foot.

Things you should know for the days ahead:

1. The revival will have an ebb and flow, like a wave pattern.

2. The revival will not take place in one city (like Toronto/ Brownsville) but will be sustained in multiple hubs and will be spread by the saints.

3. The leaders will be training and equipping others like generals in an army.

4. California will be an ignition state—wildfires of each movement will occur up and down the coast that will spread across the nation into revolution.

5. Baptism in water + fire is catalytic fuel for the wildfire of revival.

REVIVAL 101

There are many definitions and ideas about revival floating around in Christian communities. I know I have wrestled with these ideas and definitions for several years. While many people may share their thoughts and opinions on social media, that doesn't necessarily mean it's true. It is simple to water down real revival to match our experiences and to make ourselves feel better.

But, isn't revival normal Christianity? You may ask. Well, based on what definition of normal Christianity? If that means biblical Christianity, then yes. If that means living life for yourself, being consumer minded, lukewarm, and trying to fit into culture—aka most of American Christianity—then no.

We need revival because so many in the Church have forgotten their first love. We need revival because we are distracted, we are tossed by every wind of doctrine, and we need to be cut to the heart and cry out, "What must I do, Lord?"

A few months ago, I preached about the need for revival in America. Someone passively said, "Isn't this just normal Christianity." I'll be honest, remarks like this frustrate me. It's easy to dismiss the hard labor required for revival with passive arguments like such. Consequently, here we are, churches full of Christians who need reviving, who need revival.

We are in the beginning of revival and it's easy to want to move on. To take the bait and fast-forward and want to get past the long nights of prevailing prayer, the Gospel raids, the sacrifices and cost, and move into awakening, renaissance, and reformation. But hear me, we will not see reformation in the land until we are *all in* for revival. We will not see awakening till we burn for revival, and the saints are consumed to preach the Gospel.

We need to burn for revival until there is evidence to our statements. That being said, when I write about revival, what do I mean? In *Wildfires*, I break down the definition of revival based on the study and experiences of Charles Finney—leader of the Second Great Awakening in the United States. During the victories and hardships of leading

Saturate, I became enthralled by the teachings of Charles Finney. His book *Revivals of Religion* has helped guide and shape the decisions we have made in our ministry, as I consider myself to be one of his students.

Since writing *Wildfires,* I have found additional studies and resources that I believe guide us in the right direction toward real revival, how to discern if we are in one, and what to do when we are. The following are a few quotes, excerpts, and studies I have found that develop a great framework for us to begin. I encourage you to keep learning, stay hungry, and remain teachable.

WE ARE IN THE BEGINNING OF REVIVAL AND IT'S EASY TO WANT TO MOVE ON.

IN AN INSTANT GRATIFICATION CULTURE, WE CAN'T MICROWAVE A MOVE OF GOD.

WHAT IS REAL REVIVAL?

Well-known and respected preacher Charles H. Spurgeon (1834-1892) wrote, "Revival is to live again, to receive again a life which has almost expired, to rekindle into a flame the vital spark which was nearly extinguished."[1]

Hebrews 12 gives an incredible framework for revival. I often find myself meditating on the chapter and seeking the Holy Spirit for deeper insight and revelation.

> *Therefore, since we are surrounded by such a great cloud of witnesses, let us throw off everything that hinders and the sin that so easily entangles. And let us run with perseverance the race marked out for us, fixing our eyes on Jesus, the pioneer and perfecter of faith. For the joy set before him he endured the cross, scorning its shame, and sat down at the right hand of the throne*

of God. Consider him who endured such opposition from sinners, so that you will not grow weary and lose heart.

(Hebrews 12:1-3 NIV)

John Piper, a reformed American theologian wrote:

In the history of the Church, the term *revival* in its most biblical sense has meant a sovereign work of God in which the whole region of many churches, many Christians has been lifted out of spiritual indifference and worldliness into conviction of sin, earnest desires for more of Christ and his word, boldness in witness, purity of life, lots of conversions, joyful worship, renewed commitment to missions. You feel God has moved here. And basically revival, then, is God doing among many Christians at the same time or in the same region, usually, what he is doing all the time in individual Christian's lives as people get saved and individually renewed around the world.[2]

Charles Finney explains:

[Revival] presupposes that the church is sunk down in a backslidden state, and a revival consists in the return of the church from her backslidings, and in the conversion of sinners.

1. The foundations of sin need to be broken up. A revival always includes conviction of sin on the part of the church. Backslidden professors cannot wake up and begin right away in the service of God without deep searchings of heart.

The fountains of sin need to be broken up. In a true revival, Christians are always brought under such conviction; they see their sins in such a light, that often they find it impossible to maintain a hope of their acceptance with God. It does not always go to that extent, but there are always, in a genuine revival, deep convictions of sin, and often cases of abandoning all hope.

2. Revival is a new beginning of obedience with God. Just as in the case of a converted sinner, the first step is a deep repentance, a breaking down of heart, a getting down into the dust before God, with humility, and a forsaking of sin.

3. Backslidden Christians will be brought to repentance. *A revival is nothing else than a new beginning of obedience to God....*[3]

An Web search brought up the following interesting facts about revival:

Revival refers to a spiritual reawakening from a state of dormancy or stagnation in the life of a believer. It encompasses the resurfacing of a love for God, an appreciation of God's holiness, a passion for His Word and His church, a convicting awareness of personal and corporate sin, a spirit of humility, and a desire for repentance and growth in righteousness. Revival invigorates and sometimes deepens a believer's faith, opening his or her eyes to the truth in a fresh, new way. It generally involves the connotation of a fresh start with a clean slate, marking a new beginning of a life lived in obedience to God. Revival breaks the charm and power of the world, which blinds the eyes of men, and generates both the will and power to live in the world but not of the world.

In the USA, the first revival, also called the First Great Awakening, produced an upsurge of devotion among Protestants in the 1730s and 1740s, carving a permanent mark on American religion. It resulted from authoritative preaching that deeply moved the church members with a convicting awareness of personal guilt and the awesome nature of salvation through Christ. Breaking away from dry ritual and rote ceremony, the Great Awakening made Christianity intensely personal to the average person, as it should be, by creating a deep emotional need for relationship with Christ.

Revival, in many respects, replicates the believer's experience when he or she is saved. It is initiated by a prompting of the Holy Spirit, creating an awareness of something missing or wrong in the believer's life that can only be righted by God. In turn, the Christian must respond from the heart, acknowledging his or her need. Then, in a powerful way, the Holy Spirit draws back the veil the world has cast over the truth, allowing the believers to fully see themselves in comparison to God's majesty and holiness. Obviously, such comparisons bring great humility, but also great awe of God and His truly amazing grace (Isaiah 6:5). Unlike the original conversion experience that brings about a new relationship to God, however, revival represents a restoration of fellowship with God, the relationship having been retained even though the believer had pulled away for a time.[4]

HOW DO WE HAVE REVIVAL?

Charles Finney wrote:

> God has overthrown, generally, the theory that revivals are miracles. …some people are terribly alarmed at all direct efforts to promote a revival, and they cry out, "You are trying to get up a revival in your own strength. Take care, you are interfering with the sovereignty of God. Better keep along in the usual course, and let God give a revival when he thinks it is best. God is a sovereign, and it is very wrong for you to attempt to get up a revival, just because *you think* a revival is needed." This is just such preaching as the devil wants. And men cannot do the devil's work more effectually, than by preaching up the sovereignty of God, as a reason why we should not put forth efforts to produce a revival….[5]

As I have studied revival, there are four key elements that are required for revival to happen, and without them, there will not be a revival:

1. We must recognize our need for revival.

2. We must have prevailing prayer for revival.

3. There must be vessels of revival.

4. God will sovereignly raise up and send out revivalists.

The following is a letter from Evan Roberts to Miss Elsie Phillips in 1904 before the Welsh Revival. I found this letter incredibly encouraging as I felt this need to always "prove" that revival is happening. Whether it be on the beaches of California or in fields in Kentucky, there was always a comment about how it wasn't revival because ____ happened during this or that revival. I pray this letter from Evan Roberts helps you to not neglect what God is doing now:

> ...We began this mission Monday night, and we hold a prayer meeting every night at eight p.m. These meetings have been a success The young people say that they could sit all night. Monday night I explained to them the object of the mission. Then I told them of the work the Spirit was and is doing at New Quay and Newcastle-Emlyn and urged them to prepare for the baptism of the Holy Spirit. Now, this is the plan I have taken under the guidance of the Holy Spirit — There are four things to be right:
>
> (1) If there is some sin or sins in the past not confessed, we cannot have the Spirit. Therefore, we must search, and ask the Spirit to search us.
>
> (2) If there is something doubtful in our life, it must be removed — something we say of it we do not know whether it is wrong or right. This thing must be removed.
>
> (3) Total surrender to the Spirit. We must do and say all He asks us.
>
> (4) Public confession of Christ. These are the four things leading us to the grand blessing. This is our success this week in public confession — Monday night, 16, Tuesday, 6, Wednesday, 4, Thursday, 20, Friday, 19 — Total, 65.[6]

Evan believed that he was in the midst of revival by 65 souls returning to the Lord in repentance.

Have our eyes grown dim to see the revival light breaking forth. Evans regularly encouraged corporate prayer for revival.

I am asking you now, *Every morning at 9 a.m., will you join me and pray several times, for America: "Send the Spirit now, for Jesus Christ's sake."*

WHAT DO WE DO WHEN WE ARE IN REVIVAL?

From my research, I am pondering with the question: should we want sustained "revival" in our churches? I wonder if the better language is: do we want revived people in our churches; who no longer need to be revived once again because through spiritual maturity our hearts stay burning? Perhaps we keep needing revival in every generation, because we have not made disciples that are on fire for Jesus? Over the last two years, I've seen a lot of opinions and theories when it comes to revival, and unfortunately many of them are not true. The following are some helpful teachings I have found about what to do *during* revival:

> When we allow the Lord to restore a believer, very soon their family, companions, and neighbors get a portion of that benefit; for when a Christian is resuscitated and revived, they pray more intensely for sinners. ...For a congregation that continually requires restoration and revival, it is a sign of possibly false teaching, unchallenging words, or lack of encouragement. A church congregation should be a camp of fighters, not a clinic of invalids.[7]

Charles Spurgeon taught:

Those who have no spiritual life are not, and cannot be, in the strictest sense of the term, the subjects of a revival. Many blessings may come to the unconverted in consequence of a revival among Christians, but the revival itself has to do only with those who already possess spiritual life. There must be vitality in some degree before there can be a quickening of vitality, or, in other words, a revival.

A true revival is to be looked for in the church of God. Only in the river of gracious life can the pearl of revival be found. It has been said that a revival must begin with God's people; this is very true, but it is not all the truth, for the revival itself must end as well as begin there. The results of the revival will extend to the outside world, but the revival, strictly speaking, must be within the circle of life, and must therefore essentially be enjoyed by the possessors of vital godliness, and by them only. Is not this quite a different view of revival from that; which is common in society; but is it not manifestly the correct one?

It is a sorrowful fact that many who are spiritually alive greatly need reviving. It is sorrowful because it is a proof of the existence of much spiritual evil. A man in sound health with every part of his body in a vigorous condition does not need reviving. He requires daily sustenance, but reviving would be quite out of place. If he has not yet attained maturity growth will be most desirable, but a hale hearty young man wants no reviving, it would be thrown away upon him. Who thinks of reviving the noonday sun, the ocean at its flood, or the year at its prime? The tree planted by the rivers of water loaded with fruit needs not excite our anxiety for its revival, for its fruitfulness and beauty charm every one. Such should be the constant condition of the sons of God. Feeding and lying down in green pastures and led by the still waters they ought not always to be crying, "my leanness, my leanness, woe unto me." Sustained by gracious promises and enriched out of the fullness which God has treasured up in his dear Son, their souls should prosper and be in health, and their piety ought to need no reviving. They should aspire to a higher blessing, a richer mercy, than a mere revival. They have the nether springs already; they should earnestly cover the upper springs. They should be asking for growth in grace, for increase of strength, for greater success; they should have out-climbed and out-soared the period in which they need to be constantly crying, "Wilt thou not revive us again?"

For a church to be constantly needing revival is the indication of much sin, for if it were sound before the Lord it would remain in the condition into which a revival would uplift its members. A church should be a camp of soldiers, not an hospital of invalids. But there is exceedingly much difference between what ought be and what is, and consequently many of God's people are in so sad a state that the very fittest prayer for them is for revival. Some Christians are, spiritually, but barely alive. When a man has been let down into a vat or into a well full of bad air, yea do not wonder when he is drawn up again that he is half-dead, and urgently requires to be revived. Some Christians—to their shame be it spoken!—descend into such worldly company, not upon such unhallowed principles, and become so carnal, that when they are drawn up by God's grace from their backsliding position they want reviving, and even need that their spiritual breath should as it were be breathed into their nostrils afresh by God's Spirit.[8]

Day in and day out, I find the teachings of Charles Finney continuously convicting me to step out and obey over and over again. Another of his writings:

I have no idea of a preaching about revivals. It is not my design to preach so as to have you able to say at the close: "We understand all about revivals now," while you do nothing. Will you follow the instructions I shall give you from the Word of God, and then put them in practice in your own lives? Will you bring them to bear upon your families, your acquaintance, neighbors, and through the city? Or will you spend the time in learning about revivals, and do nothing for them? I want you as fast as you learn anything on the subject of revivals, to put it in practice, and go to work and see if you cannot promote a revival among sinners here. If you will not do this, I wish you to let me know at the beginning, so that I need not waste my strength. You ought to decide now whether you will do this or not. You know that we call sinners to decide on the spot whether they will obey the Gospel. And we have no more authority to let you take time to deliberate whether you will obey God, than we have to let sinners do so. We call on you to unite now in a solemn pledge to God, that you will do your duty as fast as you learn what it is, and to pray that He will pour out His Spirit upon this Church and upon all the city.[9]

Endnotes

1. C.H. Spurgeon, "What Is a Revival?" *The Spurgeon Archive, Sword and Trowel*, December 1866; https://archive.spurgeon.org/s_and_t/wir1866.php; accessed August 15, 2022.

2. DesiringGod.com, "What Is Revival and Where Do We Find It?" Ask Pastor John (Piper) Interview; https://www.desiringgod.org/interviews/what-is -revival-and-where-do-we-find-it; accessed August 15, 2022.

3. Charles Finney, "What Is Revival?"; HarvestNet.org; http://www.harvestnet .org/revival/whatisrevival.htm; accessed August 15, 2022. (Emphasis mine.)

4. "What is Christian revival?"; GotQuestions.org; https://www.gotquestions .org/Christian-revival.html; accessed August 15, 2022.

5. Charles Grandison Finney, "Lectures on Revival, Lecture I"; CharlesFinney. com; http://www.charlesfinney.com/finney/pdf/Lectures_on_Revival_by_ Charles_Finney.pdf; accessed August 15, 2022.

6. D.M. Phillips, "Evan Roberts: XXVI. The Epistles Of The Dawn Of The Revival At Laughor (cont.)"; The Welsh Revival; August 15, 2022; http:// welshrevival.org/biographies/phillips/26.htm; accessed August 15, 2022.

7. Chris Swanson, "What Is the Significance of Revival for Believers?"; Christianity.com; February 24, 2022; https://www.christianity.com/wiki/ church/what-is-the-significance-of-revival-for-believers.html; accessed August 15, 2022.

8. C.H. Spurgeon, "What Is a Revival?"; *The Spurgeon Archive, Sword and Trowel*, December 1866; https://archive.spurgeon.org/s_and_t/wir1866.php; accessed August 15, 2022.

9. Charles Grandison Finney, "Lectures on Revival, Lecture I"; CharlesFinney .com; http://www.charlesfinney.com/finney/pdf/Lectures_on_Revival_by_ Charles_Finney.pdf; accessed August 15, 2022.

3

The First Wave—Wheat, Tares, and the Remnant

Without revival, there is a very likely chance that the world in which you have grown so accustomed to will no longer exist. Historically, it only takes one generation for a nation to move from free to tyranny, and it happens swiftly like a bull thrashing its rider off its back. God is shaking things up in a nation that is easily shaken.

Let's consider the Parable of the Weeds:

> Jesus told them another parable: "The kingdom of heaven is like a man who sowed good seed in his field. But while everyone was sleeping, his enemy came and sowed weeds among the wheat, and went away. When the wheat sprouted and formed heads, then the weeds also appeared. The owner's servants came to him and said, 'Sir, didn't you sow good seed in your field? Where then did the weeds come from?' 'An enemy did this,' he replied. The servants asked him, 'Do you want us to go and pull them up?' 'No,' he answered, 'because while you are

pulling the weeds, you may uproot the wheat with them. Let both grow together until the harvest. At that time, I will tell the harvesters: First collect the weeds and tie them in bundles to be burned; then gather the wheat and bring it into my barn.'"

(Matthew 13:24-30 NIV)

Before there is massive harvest, the Lord *allows* the weeds that are sown by the enemy to grow up with it. He allows both to grow together. However, there is a timing, a moment, when the Lord says, "No longer."

THE TIME OF SEPARATION IS HARVEST TIME.

During the time of separation, the Lord will speak to those who are in the harvest first. **The people to whom you should be listening and gleaning from, in the days ahead are harvesters.** The Lord will always speak *first* to those who are prioritizing souls, because they are prioritizing the will of the Father in Heaven

As my husband Parker always jokes, "We need less preachers and more practitioners!"

I believe we will see the rise of two specific characteristics of revival:

1. An increase in evangelistic tours, widespread across the nation. Mass harvest. Tent meetings and street evangelism rallies happening everywhere and multiplying.

2. Development of training centers for revivalists and reformers. Wheat in the barn.

Where the modern-day church has lacked in these areas, God is moving through a remnant that will rise up. Pioneers who will create spaces for people to not only experience the necessary baptism of the Holy Spirit, but spaces for people to be trained, hands on, to do the work of the ministry.

We were never meant to listen to feel-good messages week in and week out. This is a violation of the empowerment of the Holy Spirit. Many end-time messengers are receiving revelation of the need for Pentecost, and I am overwhelmed by the lack of fire-filled preaching. We have swung into such a sense of apathy, that any glimmer of passion in a church is being misidentified as revival.

God is certainly bringing His fire back to the altars, and I believe that churches that can get ahold of this will be part of the greatest harvest of souls. The threshing floor has come to the United States, but let us not confuse the wheat that survives this season as the harvest. It is only the beginning, these are the workers who will be thrust out.

God is raising a remnant that will go all in for revival and won't settle for only a passionate church service. We need harvest to sweep the streets through Gospel preaching with demonstrations of power, we need the saints casting out demons, and we need prophets who won't bow to culture.

HARVEST READY

Revival is a mess, and will never be contained to only our buildings. In an effort to see a sustained move of God, let us keep our eyes lifted, and remain on our front foot as we remain nimble to the Lord's leading. There are many people who will "gather the wheat" and bring it into the barn—and there will be others who train and equip them to be sent back out.

As I spent time researching more about wheat and "tares" and what this means, I found an insightful article from the Whole Grains Council. The following explains the process of farming that many of us would miss in Jesus's parable. I believe this process is prophetically indicating the era in which we currently live.

In cereal crops like wheat, rice, barley, oats and others the seed—the grain kernel we eat—grows on the plant with an inedible hull (also sometimes called a husk) surrounding it. Before we can eat the grain kernel, we need to remove that inedible hull. This can require two processes: threshing (to loosen the hull) and winnowing (to get rid of the hull).

In some harvest-ready grains, the hull is thin and papery, and easy to remove. Little or no threshing is required, as the hull is already loose. Traditionally, farmers would toss this kind of grain into the air, from big flat baskets, letting the thin hulls—called chaff in Middle English—blow away in the wind, or fall through the chinks in the basket. This wind-assisted process for separating the wheat from the chaff is called winnowing and the grains with almost no hull are called "naked" grains.

Other grains, even when they're ripe, have a thick hull that adheres tightly to the grain kernel; these are called "covered" grains and threshing (hulling) them is a real challenge. In the old days, covered grains were often pounded to loosen the hull, or soaked in water; sometimes they even needed to be lightly milled to remove the hull.[1]

Before we can fully reap the rewards, blessings, and favor that the Lord wants to pour out as we gather the harvest, we need to remove what surrounds it. The Lord will allow *two* processes during this season—threshing and winnowing. I have been screaming from the pulpit, "If you are a ministry leader living in sin, repent while you can!"

The first wave of revival that we are currently experiencing is likened to the "harvest-ready grains." Little or no threshing is required. I love that the Whole Grains Council describes it as the chaff would "blow away in the wind." A wind-assisted process.

*H*OLY SPIRIT WINDS ARE BLOWING ACROSS THE UNITED STATES OF AMERICA.

I believe the winds of the Holy Spirit are blowing across the United States of America. The year 2020 was the beginning of a fresh wind bringing in a harvest and threshing that was already loose. While we did experience massive harvest, social media feeds filled with baptisms and outdoor gatherings, and mass exposure in the church and in our government—this was just the beginning.

As we continue to see the wind blow, other grains become visible. According to research, only 24 percent of Americans consider themselves "born again." There are still many people to reach both *in and out* of the local church. As explained in the article, I liken these people to "covered grains," and the threshing will be a real challenge. **I believe that this "baptism revival" sweeping America is loosening the hull.** When the grain is soaked in water, it helps with the removal of the hard hull. We are witnessing unprecedented numbers of deliverances during our baptism events. Demons can't stand the threshing in the water. Our hearts have become hardened and the baptism waters are an invitation to be born again and remove the former things.

> *These are the words of him who holds the seven spirits of God and the seven stars. I know your deeds; you have a reputation of being alive, but you are dead. Wake up! Strengthen what remains and is about to die, for I have found your deeds unfinished in the sight of my God. Remember, therefore, what you have received and heard; hold it fast, and repent. But if you do not wake up, I will come like a thief, and you will not know at what time I will come to you.*
>
> (Revelation 3:1-3 NIV)

Endnote

1. "Separating the Wheat from the Chaff," September 24, 2014, Oldways Whole Grains Council; https://wholegrainscouncil.org/blog/2014/09/separating -wheat-chaff; accessed August 15, 2022.

4

A New Era of Church

In 2018, I shared a blog post titled, "A Major Shift is Happening in the Global Church." I wrote quickly on the blog and explained what I was processing:

> Over the last 3-4 years, I have seen God do a shift within American Christianity. As I open up Scripture and read the Gospels, I feel an unsettling in my spirit with churches that resemble concerts or business conferences. In a desire to not be divisive and maintain unity, I have continued to pray for our churches and leaders while helping, encouraging, and investing into churches that I believe are advancing God's Kingdom.

THE CHURCH AS AN EMBASSY

A while ago, Victoria, who leads one of our Orange County churches, said that she believed God was turning our home (the Green family home) into a "Heaven Embassy." She shared that it would be a place where people could come, find refuge, and see the benefits of the Kingdom. I loved this word, because our house is where we host one of our churches. We call our house "The Green House," because people can grow and come alive in Christ here, on our couch.

Not much later, while working on my computer while at a coffee shop, I overheard one young man say to another, "Yes, that's the problem with the church. It looks too much like the world. I think the church is supposed to serve more like an embassy."

My heart started to burn as I believed that this was a word God was giving the Church!

An embassy is where an ambassador of another nation actually lives—which is a small confirmation on the micro-church movement happening and rise of house churches. An embassy promotes its own home culture, economy, and science in its host country. The embassy also protects the citizens and ambassadors living within the embassy—a home away from home.

The apostle Paul states in 2 Corinthians 5:20 (NIV), "*We are therefore Christ's ambassadors, as though God were making his appeal through us. We implore you on Christ's behalf: Be reconciled to God.*" And Philippians 3:20 (NIV) says, "*But our citizenship is in heaven. And we eagerly await a Savior from there, the Lord Jesus Christ.*"

These verses speak to the fact that the spiritual, invisible realm *is* real and is where born-again believers belong. If our citizenship is in Heaven, and we are Christ's ambassadors, that means that our homes and churches are embassies of the Kingdom of Heaven.

A SHIFT IN THE CHURCH

I think the Church is being realigned into its original intent, which is a place to equip believers to *go into all the world.* I believe that mass salvations and altar calls will begin to happen more frequently on the streets, in our offices, and in public spaces such as beaches and open fields. I believe that God is shifting the Church to reflect the economy of Heaven (generous, blessed, and sacrificial), the culture of Heaven (full of love, reverent worship, honoring authority, committed to one another), and the science of the Kingdom (healings, miracles, signs, wonders, and power). When this shift happens, church leaders will no longer have a need for "seeker friendly" services and/or attractional church models because the local church will be a reflection of what the world is truly looking for—Jesus.

Ministers, you may get 10,000 likes on social media for sharing how blessed someone will be, which is great! However, we need the voices that are crying out in the wilderness, "MAKE STRAIGHT *the way* for the Lord!"

Evangelists, this is your hour. Don't miss it. It's time to train, train, train, train, and keep training people to share the Gospel. God's thrusting out workers.

Apostles, empower the saints to take the Kingdom into every sphere! Nowhere is off limits. Apostolize! That includes wherever there are people: media, politics, education—everywhere!

Prophets, preach the uncompromised Word of the Lord. Move in power. Don't look like the rest of the world.

Teachers, study theology, learn from other streams, equip the saints to meditate on the Word of God, and learn how to be a practitioner.

Pastors, love your congregations into repentance. Identify the unique calling on their lives and help them to eat well, practice spiritual disciplines, love their family, and create order in their home and hearts.

> It is sad, sad work—painfully, dolorously, horribly sad, but saddest of all if we do not feel it to be sad, if we can go on preaching and remain careless concerning the truths we preach, indifferent as to whether men are saved or lost! May God deliver every minister from abiding in such a state! Can there be a more wretched object than a man who preaches in God's name truths which he does not feel, and which he is conscious have never impressed his own heart? To be a mere sign-post, pointing out the road but never moving in it, is a lot against which every tame heart may plead night and day.[1]

Endnote

1. C.H. Spurgeon, "What Is a Revival?"; *The Spurgeon Archive, Sword and Trowel*, December 1866; https://archive.spurgeon.org/s_and_t/wir1866.php; accessed August 15, 2022.

5

The Second Wave— Resurrection of the Unborn

ESTHER'S AND DEBORAH'S RISE

REPENTANCE OF WORSHIPPING MOLECH

Early in the fall of 2020, I was spending time in the prayer room in our house, holding our six-month-old baby girl, Summer.

I heard the Lord say, "What would you do to save her?"

I said, "Lord, anything."

He said, "What if a policy was passed that said the government could take her and kill her at any time."

I said "I would never allow it! I would protect her with my life and would fight anyone who tried to take her away from me."

The following week, when I had the vision of seven waves crashing into the United States, I heard the Lord say, "The second wave is the resurrection of the unborn."

To be clear, this is not language I use in everyday life. I mean, when go out to get a coffee, I'm not throwing around words like "resurrection of the unborn." To be honest, when I heard the word spoken to me, I had no grid for what God was talking about.

It is so important to sit, pray, and meditate on the things God is speaking to you. It is okay to ask questions and seek deeper revelation. As I prayed and processed this word, the Lord began to speak to me about the power of testimony. As the testimonies of women—who have had abortions and then have been saved, forgiven, and set free— go forth, these testimonies will release resurrection power! Where the enemy brought death, the Lord says, "I will bring LIFE!"

THE ESTHER MOVEMENT

There is an "Esther movement" arising, but the women are not who you think. God wants to bring *truth* and *passion* back into conservative Christians across America. In the days ahead, you will see a fresh anointing come upon women who have had abortions. This Esther movement isn't giving women the opportunity for a new preaching circuit, these aren't the women who feel called to preach and haven't found their place. This is not a new wave of Christian feminism.

The Esther movement is the voice that has been silenced through shame—ironically by the people who need her voice the most—the voice that has been silenced by the Church.

I believe that some of the new Esthers movement women are holding the keys to the truth about abortion through their honest experience and testimony. They are the ones afraid to speak because they may be rejected. They are the ones shaking at the thought while reading this.

However, the power of their testimony will release the angelic in such a profound and powerful way that it will shake this nation.

Statistically, 1 in 4 women are part of this Esther movement. Can you imagine the power of this collective voice? I believe that we will see the curse of abortion come off our nation, and a new Jesus movement arise of women who were once partners with the plans of the enemy—but will now be spies in the land for victory!

There is an innate trait in a woman to protect her children. Ask any mother. Abortion violates what is natural and replaces it with the demonic and the spirit of death. There is a role that the Christian woman plays that simply *cannot* be filled by a man in this movement. Men, I implore you to support, encourage, and protect these women who are speaking up for those who can't speak for themselves—the unborn children.

In the biblical story of Esther, her uncle Mordecai encourages her to speak up to protect her people. Esther's afraid to speak, but her uncle encourages her by saying these well-known words, *"For if you remain silent at this time, relief and deliverance for the Jews will arise from another place, but you and your father's family will perish. And who knows but that you have come to your royal position for such a time as this?"* (Esther 4:14 NIV).

I believe that many men are being mantled with this Mordecai anointing. His words, are now some of the most famous verses in history *"for such a time as this."* There is a rise of men who are strong, wise, and discerning—who know how to protect women as they overcome a culture that has every plan to destroy the family unit.

Here is the reality, God will raise up and protect the unborn. *This is His will.* However, this is also the hour for the Church to speak and train their congregations on healing, deliverance, and how to prioritize, love, and nurture the family unit.

DEBORAH AND ESTHER WILL HOLD HANDS

The Deborahs in this next wave are the female, uncompromised prophets whom God is unleashing with a fresh anointing as judges and defenders. The Deborahs will strategically hold hands with the Esthers and lead the charge of protecting the unborn.

A few weeks after I saw the wave vision, I had a strange dream that I am still processing to this day.

In the dream, there were several women in a coffee shop talking with one another, which was creating an echo. It sounded almost like whales talking. Jane Hamon was talking to younger women with the whale sounds as well. When I had the dream, I had only met Jane Hamon once prior, and I didn't know much about her or her ministry. So, it was a bit unusual for her to be in my dream.

I wrote down the dream and began to process it to learn what God was showing me.

I believe that Jane Hamon represents mature female prophets. I believe that there will be a synergy of generations not competing with one another but building one another up in love. I believe the generations that have gone before, that have developed their prophetic anointing, will become mothers and will hold hands with Esther as she speaks up for the voiceless, the unborn.

The last thing I will share about this wave is that I saw it crash onto the shore, it expanded further out than the other waves. I believe that as the future waves will be crashing and impacting certain parts of the nation, this second waves extends out much further as a prophetic symbol of the global effect this movement will have.

Let us never forget, Jesus came to seek and save those who are lost and to destroy the works of the enemy (see Luke 19:10; 1 John 3:8 NLT).

REPENTANCE OF WORSHIPPING MOLECH

The Lord forbids all worship of idols, and specifically child sacrifices to Molech:

> *You shall not give any of your children to offer them [by fire as a sacrifice] to Molech [the god of the Ammonites], nor shall you profane the name of your God [by honoring idols as gods]. I am the Lord.*
>
> (Leviticus 18:21 AMP)

In 1 Kings we see that even King Solomon had turned away from the Lord and began worshipping foreign gods, despite being given wisdom from the Lord: *"Solomon worshiped Ashtoreth, the goddess of the Sidonians, and Molech, the detestable god of the Ammonites"* (1 Kings 11:5).

Throughout 1 and 2 Kings, we see the rise and fall of Israel and kings obey or disobey the way of the Lord. The worship of Molech was a major indicator of the depravity and disregard for life within the Israelites at the time.

> In addition to sexual rituals, Moloch worship included child sacrifice, or "passing children through the fire." It is believed that idols of Molech were giant metal statues of a man with a bull's head. Each image had a hole in the

abdomen and possibly outstretched forearms that made a kind of ramp to the hole. A fire was lit in or around the statue. Babies were placed in the statue's arms or in the hole. When a couple sacrificed their firstborn, they believed that Moloch would ensure financial prosperity for the family and future children.[1]

It goes against the character of God to bless a nation that is sacrificing its children to idols. The apostle John commands us in his first epistle to guard ourselves against idols (see 1 John 5:21 AMP). This is militant language John is using. To guard oneself against something means we take a defensive combat position in response to it. It means, we have an opinion on the matter and oppose the demonic agenda attached to idol worship.

I believe we will see widespread repentance of worshipping Molech in America. I have seen it begin already in conferences across the nation. I have seen it in my own life. I pray that this nation will repent for sacrificing our children in the womb.

Endnote

1. "Who was Moloch?" Got Questions; https://www.gotquestions.org/who -Molech.html; accessed September 7, 2022.

6

We All Have a Story We Will Never Tell

And darkness is a harsh term, don't you think?
And yet it dominates the things I see
It seems that all my bridges have been burned
But you say, "That's exactly how this grace thing works."

—Mumford & Sons, "Roll Away Your
Stone" lyrics, Glastonbury 2010

I just want to put this out there, before we even get into the nitty gritty of this chapter. I don't want to be the "abortion" preacher. I wrestled for years trying to decide if I ever would share these stories. I recognize that this chapter *will* be offensive in many circles, and frankly I just don't care. I can't care what people will think any longer.

Abortion conversations are not comfortable among the "religious elite." You know, those who have their opinions and theories stowed away into perfectly curated notebooks and repost other people's messages without any gumption or conviction of their own. Religion is a tricky and finicky thing. It's that sneaky thought that makes the crowd love a testimony of the radical redemption of a drug user, but makes us shift in our seats when someone repents of adultery or abortion.

This chapter is for people searching for life, for those wanting freedom from shame. I hope and pray that my journey can unlock you from the bondage of the secret you may have been keeping. The "if anyone found out, I'd be done for" secrets.

Abortion.

Abortion.

Abortion.

Abortion.

For each time I have listed the word above, that is the number of times I have sat on a cold metal folding chair filling out paperwork to have an abortion. It was about nine years after having my first abortion that the secret finally came out of my mouth. Did you know that you can make secret agreements with yourself, or even worse, secret agreements with satan? It's true. We do it all the time.

Secrets like, "I'll never date a person who is shorter than me," or, "I will lose ten pounds this year." Some of these agreements are good, and some create dark little caves within our souls where we hide away from the world the true testimony of who we are and what God has done. After my first abortion, I subconsciously made one of those little agreements.

"I will never let anyone know I had an abortion."

———

It was a sticky summer afternoon in Carroll Gardens, Brooklyn. I was recently engaged to Parker Green on the beach of Montauk. Parker was the campus pastor of the church I was part of in Manhattan, and we were obsessed with one another. I was all aglow with wedding planning and all the attention that comes from being newly engaged.

"I WILL NEVER LET ANYONE KNOW I HAD AN ABORTION."

A handful of leaders from our church were being trained in healing ministry and *sozo*. I had always been passionate about praying for people to be set free and was very expectant for the training. A week prior, they had given us a cheaply printed spiral bound notebook that I had already studied word for word. Before we could begin the training, the team wanted us to first experience prayer ministry for ourselves. At this point, I had been a born-again Christian for about four years and had been prayed for more times than I could count. I felt a resistance in getting "another" prayer session under my belt, yet I knew I couldn't go on in the training if I didn't sign up.

As I sat in the lead pastor's living room, waiting for my "appointment," I looked out the floor-to-ceiling windows and watched the F train pass underneath the building. My legs stuck to the leather of the couch while my short, ripped denim Levis started to cinch at my waist. I waited anxiously for the prayer team to finish their session and call my name.

Parker then walked in, confident with tiny beads of Manhattan sweat running down his forehead onto his neon blue t-shirt. He took a seat next to me and kissed me firmly and asked how I was feeling. "Good, excited, and hoping something crazy happens." I quickly replied.

I then heard the door crack open from the paint sticking to the door frame from the summer heat. An average height woman with curly brown unkempt hair called out, "Jessi" in a musical tone. I quickly stood up and walked over to the extra bedroom where my appointment would be held.

As I sat on the plastic fold-out chair, one of the women in the room handed me a box of tissues. I politely refused and smiled while thanking them both for their time and quickly uttered, "We are really excited to do healing prayer in our church…" when I was smoothly interrupted by the unkempt hair lady who briefly explained how the session would begin.

SECRETS EXPOSED

At first, it felt a bit more like a job interview than a prayer session, if I'm honest. The two women did a thorough background check of obvious unforgiveness issues, irrational fears, and any reoccurring lies I was believing. I always think it is funny when a minister asks, "Are there any lies you are believing?" I guess I think it's silly because how am I to really know. If I am believing it, then I obviously don't know that it is a lie.

However, I complied with the questioning and mentioned my ongoing list of people I was forgiving 77 x 7 times, and the women walked me through a forgiveness prayer for each one. It felt nice to choose to forgive people who hurt me, but there were no Holy Spirit goosebumps and certainly no tears.

As we continued, I began to feel really confident in my walk with God. I had done the hard work of grieving things from my past, regularly forgiving others, and constantly talking to leaders about where I was in my spiritual journey. I am always described as the "authentic" or "raw" leader, which I appreciated.

The truth is, I hate secrets. Secrets burn in my chest waiting to come out, which leads to all sorts of problems including gossip and or saying things that are misinterpreted and offend people. Yet, I wear my "authentic" badge of honor and pride myself on being an open book.

As the session was concluding, I started to take mental notes of how I would ask these same questions in a more "provoking" way perhaps. I then noticed the silent woman with the tissue box writing notes on a yellow notepad. I tried to peer over her chubby freckled arms but couldn't make out the scribbles. I boldly asked, "What are you writing?"

Then she looked up at me sheepishly. The two women exchanged glances and curly hair said, "Well, that about wraps up your session… unless there is anything else you can think of." I honestly couldn't. I thought they had done a pretty great job until the silent one handed me the piece of paper. On the paper I read: "Kings from Jessi's Womb—like Jesse in the Bible"

I felt sick. Why would God bring that up? Why now?

7

How Secrets Are Born

It was the weekend after my eighteenth birthday. I had just finished my freshman year at the University of Miami. I was home in Huntington, Long Island, visiting my parents before heading back to school. I couldn't wait for the summer to be over. My freshman year was what they write teen movies about. I was dating a senior who was president of his fraternity, and while my social status was thriving, my faith was barely hanging on. My nights were filled with 4 a.m. walks back to my dorm room across the sprinkler-soaked intramural fields that separated the fraternity houses from the freshman dorms. There was not a chance that I was going to wake up early for a "Campus Bible Study" or crawl into church and sit in a stiff wooden pew hungover and squinty eyed.

After the whirlwind of my freshman year, I decided to visit a Planned Parenthood in my hometown that summer to get birth control. I nervously walked up to the automatic glass door, afraid of being recognized by one of the country club moms who frequented the shopping complex.

Throughout high school, I strongly judged the "trashy" girls who went to Planned Parenthood. Yet here I was wanting to be somewhat responsible in my promiscuous lifestyle. As I filled out the paperwork, my high school friend, Bridgett, sat next to me and encouraged me that getting birth control was a really mature decision. I agreed, and scribbled a made-up address on the form in fear that my parents would get some kind of newsletter to their conservative home that would expose my irreligious lifestyle.

The woman at the front desk collected my papers and immediately took me to the back. The Planned Parenthood in my conservative hometown is not exactly overflowing with patients in the waiting room. The town is both traditional in their values and most families are financially well off. The mailboxes that lined the suburban streets never received applications for people seeking medical assistance, and there is a horse and buggy that brings mothers with their children to the stores throughout Main Street during Christmastime. The entrance sign of my hometown states "A great place to work, play, and raise a family"— and that is not a lie.

As I walked toward the back of the Planned Parenthood complex, I was handed a cup to fill with urine and place into a stainless steel metal box in the floral-walled bathroom. I then headed to the examination room where the doctor asked me the preliminary questions that would qualify me for $30 birth control pills without my parents' consent and insurance. As I sat on the table, I answered the questions quickly, and desperately wanted to be finished with the appointment.

DENIED BIRTH CONTROL

The whole conversation was grating to my Christian upbringing. Discussing with a complete stranger my lifestyle choices felt too exposing, as I had to come face to face with the poor decisions of my last year. As the doctor left the office to write my prescription, I patiently tapped my bare feet on the cold metal chair and read the posters on the wall about various STDs.

I went into the clinic to get a pregnancy test for birth control and then the nurse came in to tell me that I was in fact pregnant and they could not write me a birth control prescription. Honestly, I freaked out and was so nervous about my parents finding out. My mom raised me as a single parent and I grew up hearing stories of all of the sacrifices she had made for me. I had so many dreams and ambitions and with this new "news," I saw my entire future quickly going down the drain. I curled up and just began to weep. The nurse didn't skip a beat and quickly gave me my options for an abortion. I was past the point to take the morning after pill and would need to make an appointment for a surgical abortion as soon as possible.

ALONE.

I was only 18 years old and was riddled with fear. Fear of being alone, fear of what people may think, fear of my parents, fear about finances, and fear of losing my boyfriend. These organizations that say they advocate for the rights of women were not advocating for me or for the life of my unborn child. I was never given options for counseling or referred to a clinic to discuss the myriad of options that I had. I could barely decide where to go out for dinner on a Friday night. The decision of what to do with the life of a child was overwhelming. My options were I could have an abortion or do research to give the child up for adoption and face more rejection and shame.

About a week later, I ended up telling my boyfriend. He freaked out for a few moments and then encouraged me that we would be okay. That we could figure this out together. Hope slowly began to rise. Maybe I could keep the baby and my boyfriend and I could begin a simple and humble life together in Florida. I began running millions of scenarios through my mind and thought, *Maybe I could actually keep this baby.*

That Sunday, I reluctantly agreed to go to church with my parents. I sat quietly in the pew as the congregation sang, "Heart of Worship." Although I was in church, I couldn't have felt farther from God or more alone. I slipped out the back door to take "a quick call" from my boyfriend's mom. She was a cool, edgy, liberal mom, and my boyfriend decided to tell her about our "situation" because it was all too big for us. On the phone, she lovingly expressed how thankful she was that I was dating her son and how heartbroken she was to hear our news. Without getting into all the details, she strongly encouraged me to go through the simple procedure of an abortion and not "ruin our future."

Alone, again.

My boyfriend agreed with his mother, so we were back to the drawing board. I ended up looking back to the "resources" Planned Parenthood gave me for an "in-clinic abortion." The medical staff could make the whole process as "comfortable as possible." The pamphlet encouraged me that "I could return to my normal activities" following the abortion. I was told "having an abortion is simple, common and safe." It was much harder to get an abortion after 12 weeks, so if this is a decision I wanted to make, I needed to make it quickly.

CHEAP CATTLE

I could no longer handle the pressure from my boyfriend, his mother, and the tormenting thoughts that haunted me day in and day out. I made an appointment at the nearest clinic and was in the waiting room within a few days. The waiting room was cold and sterile—the wall was lined with metal folding chairs filled with quiet women. No one talked in that waiting room.

As I began to fill out my paperwork, I had a panic attack. I couldn't do this. I couldn't go through with this. I would keep the baby, even if I was by myself. I ran to the front desk in tears and handed them my clipboard. I ran into the parking lot and cried out in agony. "Why is this happening to me? Why was I so stupid?!" I went back into the office and wiped my tears on my jacket sleeve. The woman at the front desk told me that I could not have fits like that because it was "disrupting" the other patients.

It is probably a longer story for another book, but I ended up having the "procedure." The process was anything but "simple, common and safe." After the abortion, I was placed in a cold, metal folding chair, bleeding out onto a maxi pad and dozing in and out from the anesthesia. I briefly opened my eyes to see the other women across from me. I felt like cheap cattle in a slaughter house. Then my body fell forward and my face smashed against the cold, white linoleum floor. A nurse came over and propped me up into the chair again, readjusted the hospital gown, and snapped her fingers in front of my face, barking, "Wake up! Wake up!"

DISAPPEAR.

But waking up was the very last thing I wanted to do. I wanted to sleep. To slip away. To disappear and never resurface again to face the decision I made. I killed a baby. I killed my baby. They forgot to mention the grief that overwhelms the depths of your soul when you make a decision like that.

The fear didn't go away, it only increased and now had a new partner called shame. The door was now officially open for a lifestyle of numbing myself from my thoughts. Cocaine addictions followed. Anything to keep me from being alone, not in my room, tormented by horrific thoughts. *How could God forgive me?* Maybe I didn't want to follow a God who would.

———

"Abortion is murder. Period," said the young associate pastor in the car seat in front of me. It took about all of my restraint to not strangle her around the neck with my gold satin headband. There were about eight of us women crammed into a black Suburban driving to Virginia Beach from New York City. I was squished in the third row, which really isn't a row if you ask me. Two of my closest friends were sitting with me, our legs intertwined resembling the top crust of a homemade apple pie.

Our lead pastor was speaking at a women's conference, and a group of us went to enjoy a weekend away in the warm Virginia sun and cheer her on as she preached. The theme for the conference was "Freedom," and many of the women in the car were discussing areas and topics they thought may be brought up.

As I was editing a photo on my phone, I overheard someone in the front bring up the topic of abortion. I reached into my bag to pull out my smart water and slowly sipped as I felt my throat closing up and my face begin to get hot.

"Abortion is murder. Period."

Those words rang through my ears, down the veins in my neck, right through the very tip of my fingernails. I lifted my sweatshirt up to my chin, sure that my friends would be able to see my veins heavily pulsating. As adrenaline rushed in, my body was preparing for fight or flight. Yet, there I was, stuck in that stupid third row with nowhere to go. It was now four years since having my fourth abortion, and I felt the shame of every bad decision of my past sweeping over me like a tidal wave. I crunched down and hid my phone between my black leggings and quickly texted my husband, Parker, about what just happened. I concluded the story with, "This is why I hate Christians and this is why I will never, ever tell anyone."

THE REALITY OF DEATH AND GRIEF

I quickly saw a grey speech bubble pop up on my phone. Parker replied "She's an a-hole. Don't let her get to you. She wouldn't know compassion if it punched her in the face." I closed my eyes and slowly pictured myself punching her in the face.

What pains me is that this is probably not the first conversation like this. I think it is important for me to clarify that I am *for* women carrying to full term, delivering their baby, and either keeping or giving up the child for adoption. However, the reality is that statistically one in three women are in fact having abortions. In hundreds of cases in churches around the globe, after an altar call I have been the first person someone has told about their abortion secret.

Worldwide, pastors, leaders, mentors, and peers are choosing to fight for the lives of the unborn children while destroying the lives of the living. We can all do better. Me included. I can't tell you how many conferences I have been to where everyone watched a beautifully curated video of former drug addicts who turned their lives around, became clean, and now follow Jesus. Yet when a woman shares from the stage that she has had an abortion or committed adultery, the room becomes so still that you could hear a communion wafer hit the carpeted floor.

> ...*Because Jesus was raised from the dead, we've been given* **a brand-new life** *and have everything to live for,* **including a future in heaven**—*and the future starts now! God is keeping careful watch over us and the future. The Day is coming when you'll have it all—life healed and whole.*
>
> (1 Peter 1:3-5 The Message)

This Scripture passage stirs something deep within me, and I pray the Holy Spirit speaks to you now as well. It is a glimpse of what our souls long for. The Gospel is only Good News if you believe it. The truth is, when God created humans, we were meant to have an intimate relationship with Him. It says that Adam walked with God in the cool of the day. However, when Eve and Adam were deceived, sin entered the world. I think it is important to note that they were in fact deceived.

Many of us have the ability to fully access all the things of God, but many of us never get there because of this same deception. When sin entered the world, it separated us from a Holy God. This feels unfair, but as I have learned to love God, I understand that this was more unfair to Him than us. The fact that God sent His Son, Jesus, to come to earth as a man, live a sinless life, die on a cross for my sins, and then rise from the dead is a lot to fully accept.

Our souls wrestle with if we are worthy enough to receive this kind of sacrifice. So we accept half-truths, while still holding onto our past, our pain, and our own unforgiveness. I believe that for many of us, it is easier to believe in a Jesus who would forgive us for our sins, than to follow One who rose from the dead. However, Jesus is in fact *alive* and ruling and reigning. So what does that mean for you?

SALVATION IS ACCESS.

Peter tells us that because He is alive, we have a new option. *Salvation!* I want to be clear here. Salvation is so much more than getting by into heaven. It is access, grace, power, and the full ability to live the life God created you for. Salvation is the most amazing miracle to witness, but we settle for less.

Sometime later, after that dreadful car ride to the conference, my sister-in-law was running a gathering of female leaders to pray and seek God together before her upcoming "She is Free" conference. During our time together, we were instructed to write on a postcard something Jesus had us set free from. Going through the motions, I wrote about depression and other things that are more widely accepted within church culture. As we went around the table and shared what we had written, I read my card with confidence as an overcomer. Yet when everyone was finishing up, one of the women had the courage to share something extremely vulnerable. This is a key to the revival ahead; there is a ripple that comes as we open our lives to one another and allow the Holy Spirit to reveal deep parts of us that need His healing and redemption.

In the moment of her sharing, I felt the Spirit of God wash over me and whisper, "You need to share your secret." I tried to swallow, but my saliva felt like a million rocks blocking my throat.

With every ounce of courage I had, I spoke up and said, "Wait, I need to say something."

RIPPLE EFFECT

I then unloaded about having an abortion. I hoped that in this place of vulnerability, that the other women present would extend forgiveness and mercy for me, this young girl who made several mistakes in her past. As I shared my secret sin, I felt a huge weight lifted from off my chest. The women surrounded me in prayer as I wept and snot ran down my face.

The next morning, I got coffee with my best friend Gracie. We sat together and I decided to tell her the whole truth. The whole experience of every abortion, every anxiety, shame, fear and depression that marked the previous years of my life.

Later that evening, my sister-in-law asked me if I would be willing to share that night at a women's ministry event about what God had been setting me free from. I wasn't sure if I could do it. I just told people my secret for the first time the day before—I didn't know if I had the courage to share it again with an entire room full of women.

My body shook like a leaf on a tree as the words came out of my mouth on that stage during the event. Afterward, we offered prayer to anyone who needed prayer. Shockingly, I ended up praying for more than ten women who had had an abortion and had never told anyone until that moment.

8

Pro-Life
Needs Rebranding

Mute Conversation"—I found myself tapping this sneaky little button in the settings of my social media account. A popular "pro-life" account was getting a bit hectic; as I scrolled my feed, it made me feel kinda "icky" for lack of a better term.

In my early twenties, the moment flickered in my mind, "Jess, just go inside the church. Someone in there can help you." Weeks before deciding to have an abortion, my mind raced back to being ostracized by the youth group for having a Jewish boyfriend while in high school and the looks of judgment for going to a Linkin Park concert.

I don't belong here. I wonder how often many women who have had abortions feel like this. The answer is, All. The. Time.

After two years of leading altar calls around the country and calling women who have had abortions to repentance and freedom, I have recognized this common thread of isolation, shame, and fear of rejection. Here is the truth, we can actually talk about sin and call people into repentance and still love them and show compassion. Do not be deceived and believe the lie that you need to keep your voice silent on difficult topics.

THE LONG GAME

The reality is, even when I was not following Jesus, I knew having an abortion was the absolute worst decision I would ever make. However, fear of rejection overrode my moral compass. Humanity has this way of creating cycles in life—downward or upward, it feels as though we are all spiraling. I was on the downward spiral. Repeat offenses.

They say, "Only an idiot makes the same decision over and over and expects a different outcome." I felt like a blonde, twenty-something idiot. An idiot who couldn't break the cycle of destruction and rejection in my life.

After Jesus wreaked havoc on my self-destructing life and offered me such supernatural inconceivable joy, I found myself wanting life instead of death. Both for myself, those around me, and for the unborn.

I'll make this blunt. Trigger the offense here. The pro-life movement is kinda cringe to me.

When women are scared, alone, broken and pregnant, and we are only communicating to them that they are murderers and should keep the baby because the science proves the fetus is a child…I just don't know how well that is going to work in the long game.

ONE PERSON

I tried a little experiment, and it worked. The result was crazy.

I was living in New York City and had met this amazing woman who was trying to get her life on track. She was in an abusive relationship and was trying to get out. A recent new believer of Jesus, she was attending church, meeting me for discipleship, and working hard and partying less. I told her, "No matter what, I'm here for you. I want you to know that." One morning she called me to go for coffee with her and said it was important that we meet.

We stepped down a dirty staircase and into a hidden coffee shop off of Irvine Street. One of my favorite things about Manhattan is the busyness of crowds, and the ability to slip away into what would appear to be a hidden oasis for those who knew how to find them.

We grabbed lattes and sat, tucked away from the cold, in a tiny corner of this below-street-level coffee shop. She put her hands over her face and began to cry. She peered over her chipped fingernail polish and whispered to me, "I'm pregnant. I don't know what to do. I'm going to get an abortion."

In that moment, I realized, *Man, it's so much easier to post about this kinda stuff on social media,* and wished I could keep swiping till I saw a funny meme.

After a moment, I grabbed her by the hand and said, "I don't think you should do that. When I had an abortion, it didn't solve anything for me. I was only riddled with more anxiety, suicidal thoughts, and depression. The guilt consumed me. You can do this. I'm here for you." As we talked back and forth, I encouraged her to make an ultrasound appointment and call me after.

I looked at my personal bank account, with a few hundred dollars, and offered to help financially in every way I could to cover expenses for the baby. We didn't do a church-wide rally, I didn't share it on Instagram, I simply took personal responsibility for the one person Jesus had brought into my path. I simply decided to try my best to help this one person.

She kept the baby. His name is Gabe.

She allowed me to invite other people I trusted into the situation. My mother-in-law Mavis, who happens to be a doula, began prayer counseling with her as well. We purchased things for the baby and she was eventually given a promotion at work. Listen, I didn't start a pro-life movement with that coffee date. However, there is another eternal soul on this earth now with a mother who feels loved, supported, and had people to walk with.

The backlash from the pro-choice movement is that conservatives don't care for the mother and child after the baby is born. That is the biggest misleading lie out there. I am not going to take up space in this book for what you could so easily research online, but Christians actually *lead* the way when it comes to adoption, foster parenting, and providing for single parents.

REBRANDING PRO-LIFE

Okay, okay, back to the chapter title and the rebranding conversation. If I rebranded pro-life, it would probably be a campaign for free massages, coffee dates, and a banquet for moms who have had abortions to be loved and set free, and for single moms to be connected to friends who will be there for them and help take care of their needs. Socialism robs us of compassion. It destroys the creative ability that God bestows to His saints to love and serve their neighbors that are right in their midst.

Please realize that you are *not* required to take care of every single mom and baby. You are *not* required to solve the world's problems. Right now, I break off of you the burden to carry the weight of national sin on your shoulders. This is a weapon the enemy uses via media to make us feel apathetic, tired, and makes it impossible to celebrate victory.

Simply lift up your eyes. Be available. Keep cash in your wallet, and ask God to highlight people for you to bless.

We need to stand in unity for the fact that abortion is wrong and it violates everything that is in your God-given nature. I pray that the Church throughout the United States will display such a compelling celebration of those who choose life, that those who are burdened by fear will be overwhelmed by the love of Jesus saying, "Come to Me, all who are weary and heavy burdened."

DISCERNMENT

The slogan of the satanic temple is "Thyself is thy master." On the satanic website it says, "Consistent with our tenets that call for bodily autonomy and acting in accordance with best scientific evidence, The satanic temple religiously objects to many of the restrictions that states have enacted that interfere with abortion access as well as other related issues that affect members' religious rights. TST is taking many steps to address reproductive laws that violate our religious conscience by inflicting guilt and shame in one's decision and being inconsistent with necessary health and safety standards."

I recently joked to a friend, "If your discernment is struggling in this season, here's a really simple tool. You don't want to be on the same page as the satanic temple if you are a follower of Jesus." Okay, so what in the world does this have to do waves, revival, awakening in America, and a prophetic showdown?

Everything.

I was driving to Charlotte, North Carolina, with my friend Vic after the overturning of Roe v. Wade in 2022, and I was in shock for two reasons:

1. I couldn't believe that the second wave was happening so quickly and things were shifting rapidly in America. The curse of abortion was being lifted off of the nation, and was now in the hands of each state.

2. The reaction of many pastors and leaders was incredibly grieving and shocking. I thought if there was ever a moment in America's history for a united Church front, this was it. Yet it appeared as if the chasm was growing wider, not smaller.

As I prayed and discussed with Vic the implications of this national moment, what it meant for revival, and our part to play, we both had an "ah ha" moment. One of my favorite truths about the prophetic is that the Word is living. As God released vision and revelation, as time continues, it invites us deeper and further into revelation and wisdom. Although I was shocked at the reaction of many church leaders, the Lord revealed to us in the car that this was all connected to the original first wave—separating the wheat and the tares.

At this moment I realized that each coming wave of revival was connected to the past and future waves. As we continued to pray and process and exclaim, "This is so CRAZY!" the Lord began to reveal to me why it must be this way. The first wave was the first shaking. Exposure on a global level. Churches shutting down while movements were being birthed. The second wave, being connected to the first, was in fact separating the wheat from the tares on a greater level. Specifically cleansing and exposing the hearts of pastors and prophets.

EACH COMING WAVE IS CONNECTED TO THE PAST AND FUTURE WAVES.

Why does this matter for revival? Pastors are meant to be shepherds and lead their congregation in "The Way." They are meant to train the saints how to navigate the culture with wisdom and discernment. They are called to love their members and help them to live fully alive and free through the gift of the Gospel of Jesus. Prophets are called to be the mouthpiece of God. They are meant to hear from Heaven, and without compromise or opinion, called to reveal the will of the Father to the people in the world.

9

Christian Witchcraft

We are created in the image of God and we have an eternal spirit within us. Often, ministries are not offering people the very supernatural life they were created for.

At 17 years old, I was hungover, and sitting on the beige cushioned pew of the Presbyterian church my parents attended. My eyes glazed over as I rested my head on my dad's shoulder. I listened to the sermon, which was a deep theological study of some book in the Bible I had never heard of. As we stood up and half-heartedly sang, "Ancient of Days," I counted down the minutes we could leave and head to the Golden Dolphin for the incredible Sunday lunch special and corn bread basket.

Unfortunately, this is a similar church experience for many Christians in America. They leave church and watch videos online of wrinkle-free, lip-filled, Louis Vuitton toting women sharing with great passion and excitement how they "manifested" their dream date with their dream guy. The gregarious content creator shares her "secrets" to the good life, the supernatural life, and all the young onlooker has to do is "think positively"! The bait seems pure and innocent enough. I mean, wouldn't

God want me to be a more positive person? There can't be anything wrong with wanting to have vision, goals, and "decreeing" that I will be blessed, this will be the year I get my dream car, my dream spouse, my dream kitchen, my dream vacation, my dream...life.

I was 21 years old when I read the book, *The Secret* by Rhonda Byrne.[1] The title peeked my interest, and anyone who knows anything about psychology understands that we all want to know secrets. As I read each chapter rather quickly, it all made perfect sense to me. I was somewhat shocked that the BIG "secret" was basically gratitude and positive thinking.

These "clues to manifesting your dream life" seemed simple enough. But alas, here I was, praying to the universe to manifest a white feather on a Monday afternoon. Then walking down 21ˢᵗ Street, right there on the pavement, there it was. A perfectly white feather. My faith in manifesting was building, and being the evangelist (by God-given nature) that I am, I began to buy the book for everyone I knew.

After some time, I began to positively thank in advance the "universe" for my $1,300 red-bottomed Christian Louboutin heels, my Louis Vuitton luggage, and dream vacations around the world. Distracted by all these glittering things, I had yet to realize that I was increasingly anxious, feeling more depressed, and had lingering thoughts and daydreams about walking into busy New York City traffic streets and ending my life. Totally normal! Deep sarcasm intended, yet this is how much of the next generation is thinking and being discipled through social media.

There is no warning label on New Age books, and the Church has been too silent on the issue. After attending church for nearly twenty-one faithful years, how had I never heard that there was *indeed* a very real and tangible spiritual realm surrounding us. That God has miracle-working power, that demons are real, and that the best life is not the one the world is promoting. I didn't realize that the spiritual principles and laws that were created by God, were being demonically used against me to make myself a small god.

THERE IS NO WARNING LABEL ON NEW AGE BOOKS, AND THE CHURCH HAS BEEN TOO SILENT ON THE ISSUE.

WITCHCRAFT WITH A JESUS STICKER

Ok, I'll repeat that for my charismatic friends, because there is a temptation that can also arise in churches to dabble in a little bit of witchcraft with a Jesus sticker on the package. I'm sorry, I'm sorry, don't throw down this book! Don't get mad, please!

Yet, we need to go there.

The idols are coming down.

Read this carefully: We were *not* created to be gods, and the moment we begin decreeing, declaring, and using our faith to make *our* will be done, and not God's will, we are opening ourselves up to the demonic.

I hate to write this so plainly, but it *is* that simple. It is so important to pray the Word of God and decree His promises. However, if we are not careful, this can easily get twisted into something very different. I particularly appreciate how Dr. David Yonggi Cho teaches on this topic in his book *Fourth Dimension*.[2] We need to pray and ask God for His vision. We need a *rhema* word, we need faith for what God is doing. Then, that is when we pray, decree, believe, and have faith in God doing that very thing. It must be God's plan first, not a carnal Christian version of our own plans.

I have recently been studying Romans 8 in-depth. It really hit me in verse 28 that says, *"God works for the good of those who love him, who have been called according to his purpose."* Sometimes you hear a verse so often that it kind of loses its "weight," and you can read it passively without paying attention. Well as I read this verse, it hit me—all things work together for good when its according to His purposes, not our own. For years, I wrestled with why it felt like God was working things out for good in everyone's life but mine. Here is a secret revealed, the golden ticket—we need to lay down our purposes for His, that's when it all works together for good.

DISCERNMENT FILTER

I never expected it to be this way, but the overturning of Roe v. Wade was another discernment filter for the days ahead. Years ago, I would play the "politically correct church game" in an effort to not be contrary or offensive. However, there is too much at stake, and too much murky water to be messing around with what sounds nice, but is destroying people's lives.

On my social media account, I made a bold statement: "Thank You, Jesus, for opening our eyes. Thank You for helping us see. If your pastor did not speak up about Roe v. Wade being overturned, you now have permission to leave that church."

The reality is, there are too many people who are staying in dry places and wondering why they are constantly struggling. They are living in places to prioritize their comfort and routine over moving and finding others to burn with. The days are short, it is much better to find your people, to get equipped and be spiritually set on fire while you may need to live in a smaller home and sell your possessions. Do whatever it takes.

Obviously not everyone is called to relocate, leave their church, or change their jobs or ministries. Don't hear what I am not saying. However, it is definitely the season to pray, fast, and get into the secret place with everything laid out before the Lord and say, "Here, God, I give You my heart, my possessions, my will, my future. What are You doing? How do I partner with You?" Then I encourage you to step out in faith and say, "Yes!" to God!

Endnotes

1. Rhonda Byrne, *The Secret* (New York: Atria Books/Beyond Words, 2006).

2. David Yonggi Cho, *The Fourth Dimension* (New Kensington, PA: Bridge-Logos Publishers, 1979). Dr. Cho (1936-2021) was the founding pastor of the world's largest church, located in Seoul, South Korea, with more than 700,000 members involved in more than 25,000 home cell groups.

10

The Third Wave—The Prophetic Showdown

But when the Helper comes, whom I will send to you from the Father, the Spirit of truth, who proceeds from the Father, he will bear witness about me. And you also will bear witness, because you have been with me from the beginning.

(John 15:26-27 ESV)

…As the Father has sent me, I am sending you.

(John 20:21 NIV)

The words in our opening Scripture passages from out of the mouth of resurrected Jesus should create pause. The first thing Jesus says to His best friends after resurrecting, the first words in the new era of Christianity are sending words. After Jesus sent them to do what He did, He breathes on them.

Brian Simmons, who has written the Passion Translation of the Bible, explains that the Greek word is used only one time in all of the

New Testament. However, it is the same word for when God breathed into Adam's nostrils in such great intimacy and released to him the breath of life (Genesis 2:7).

Later in Acts 2, the disciples receive the baptism of the Holy Spirit for power, but this baptism is for a brand-new life (Acts 2:1-4,38). From this point, Jesus says to them that *"repentance for the forgiveness of sins will be preached"* (Luke 24:46-49).

One of the markers of the ministry of Jesus was the display of authority given to Him from the Father. He offered people forgiveness for their sins, setting them free from what ultimately keeps a person in bondage. Once released from the chains of sin, they went on to receive miraculous healing, deliverance, and transformation that also transformed cities.

I wrestle with the idea at times that we want to receive the baptism of the Holy Spirit for another reason. We want His forgiveness, His presence, and His power for just about anything other than share the Gospel and release people from their sins and cast out demons. It's weird, right?

DEMONSTRATIONS OF POWER

Even worse, I am bewildered at how many churches I visit across the nations that want nothing to do with the Holy Spirit. Sure, they can't outright deny Him because that would be to forsake all of Scripture, thus they are not Christians at all. Yet in their practice, they deny and grieve the Holy Spirit. They leave no space, no area, no time of prayer or expectation for the Holy Spirit to fill people, to move them, to do something uncomfortable and off-program. I beg the question: Can we even call ourselves true believers and followers of Jesus Christ without living lives so provoked by the Holy Spirit that we *must* share the Gospel and challenge unbelievers through demonstrations of power?

I have learned one of the most difficult lessons, as a hopeful and optimistic believer. People love, like, and share on social media photos of big crowds, mass baptisms, salvations, and stadium events. I rarely see controversy online regarding these things, and get only a few hateful emails or criticisms when sharing about that. However, if you want to see the guns of the church come out blazing, share something that demonstrates the power of God. Post a photo or story of someone being healed with medical reports proving the healing, share a video of someone falling backward under the power and glory of God, show a photo of crowds laying in the mud crawling into a baptismal tank. Yeah, that kinda stuff gets all sorts of criticism. Yet, that kind of power is the revival stuff we are praying for.

> *I know your deeds, that you are neither cold nor hot. I wish you were either one or the other! So, because you are lukewarm—neither hot nor cold—I am about to spit you out of my mouth. You say, "I am rich; I have acquired wealth and do not need a thing." But you do not realize that you are wretched, pitiful, poor, blind and naked. I counsel you to buy from me gold refined in the fire, so you can become rich; and white clothes to wear, so you can cover your shameful nakedness; and salve to put on your eyes, so you can see. Those whom I love I rebuke and discipline. So be earnest and repent. Here I am! I stand at the door and knock. If anyone hears my voice and opens the door, I will come in and eat with that person, and they with me. To the one who is victorious, I will give the right to sit with me on my throne, just as I was victorious and sat down with my*

Father on his throne. Whoever has ears, let them hear what the Spirit says to the churches.

(Revelation 3:15-22 NIV)

*W*ARNING: THERE IS A PROPHETIC SHOWDOWN COMING, AND IT IS COMING SOON.

I pray this book releases before it starts to happen, in hopes that as many people as possible can navigate these times.

To my surprise, I spent several chapters of this book to break down the second wave of revival, my own story of freedom from having multiple abortions, and how to discern the times. As I shared, Roe v. Wade separated the wheat from the tares again. The prophets and pastors in this particular wave, are being shaken to a greater measure. Why?

I asked that same question myself.

After taking time to pray into the third wave of revival, I believe there is going to be a massive increase in witchcraft and demonic manifestations across the United States; and in many cases, the culture will celebrate it. You are about to witness things that you never imagined being "out in the public" not only openly being done, but being called normal. In addition to this, there is an increase in counterfeit anointing, power, and prophets that will increase in influence that are *no* different from the prophets of Baal.

At the same time, there will be a remnant of pure-hearted, consecrated prophets. I use the word remnant, this does not include everyone. These prophets have been tested through persecution from both the world and churches in the last few years, and have come through the refiners fire. They have paid a price to be firebrand. They have been gifted with a mixture of Elijah and John the Baptist anointings.

TESTING

PAY ATTENTION. I REPEAT, PAY ATTENTION.

If a prophet is not standing for life, *proceed with caution*. If a prophet is the mouthpiece of God and is afraid to rustle feathers over the topic of abortion, that person is at risk of being compromised. I am not saying these prophets are in fact compromised, but they are *at risk* because the cares of the world have entered into their hearts and minds and their pure prophetic voice is compromised.

Why do the prophets need to be tested and separated to a greater measure for what's ahead?

The testing and separation is because there is going to be the greatest anointing ever seen on earth, and it's about to come upon these consecrated prophets. I am talking about miraculous displays of the reality of God and His Kingdom. Elijah calling down fire type of things.

With the increase in witchcraft and demonic manifestation, the world will witness the controversial power of Jesus as Lord on display. I believe that many of these prophets are seeing visions of places including New York City, San Francisco, Seattle, Washington DC, Los Angeles, and Chicago.

A POWER CONFRONTATION

A vision I keep seeing is connected to this, that I feel is a prototype for the season ahead. In the vision, I see prophets Jeremiah Johnson and Tomi Arayomi linking arms and hand selecting an army to go into these specific cities and sending forth firebrand prophetic saints who are trained and equipped to hold the line. Behind the fire wall came what sounded like "rushing waters," which I believe represents Gospel-pure evangelists preaching and baptizing on the streets.

In this vision, I saw satanists, witches, and New Age "peace makers" come to the see what was happening. A power confrontation took place and the news media and police showed up because of the crowds. I heard Jeremiah yell out, "Where are your gods?" and everyone fell to the ground as people began to cry out and repent because of the very *real* tangible *fear* and *love* of the Lord that fell upon the people in these cities.

Then, the sent-in evangelists grabbed hands with the pastors who had been separated and set apart in the second wave, and they gave them a brand-new fishing net and said, "Use this instead."

Jesus, prepare us. Let it be so.

11

The Fourth Wave— National Repentance

LOVE, POWER, URGENCY, AND MASS BAPTISMS

In Sterquiliniis Invenitur is an ancient Greek phrase meaning, "In filth it will be found." Likewise, I believe that breakthrough is often found where we are least willing to look.

FALLING APART

There I was, in khaki pants and a baby blue silk shirt, on the corner of 23rd Street and 5th Avenue in New York City. My knees hit the pavement with violence as the muddy waters of filthy streets splashed over me. The rain would not stop pouring down. Each droplet cursing me as I desperately tried to hail a cab—these were the days before car services like Uber and Lyft. I witnessed one person after the other claim the yellow cab that was rightfully mine.

It had been a hard day at the office, working for a nightclub company and preparing for the upcoming holiday festivities. I was exhausted, hungover, and battling ongoing anxiety with a grey fog of depression. It was finally time to head home, which at that point was my boyfriend's apartment. At first, I tried to dodge the rain with hopes that I would quickly find a cab and avoid the mess altogether.

However, after twenty or so minutes had passed and the rain became colder, harder, and flooded the city streets, cabs became less and less available as my emotions became more and more apparent. I screamed out to the heavens, "I can't do this!" and fell apart, right there, near the Flatiron building, as busy New Yorkers rushed past me, splashing me on their way. As I cried on the ground, defeated, soaked, and feeling hopeless, I called my boyfriend. After a few rings it went to voicemail. I felt alone, stuck.

A few moments later, I began to walk toward the apartment, hoping to find a cab along the way. About seven streets into my journey, I saw two passengers leaving their taxi, so I sprinted down the busy city streets full of puddles, trash, and more dirt. I jumped into the cab and we sped down 1st Avenue toward the apartment. After paying the driver, I rushed up to the elevator and pushed the button to my floor, when the elevator opened, I pushed through to my apartment door down the hall and my frozen, wet fingers shook to unlock the deadbolt. Once I was finally inside, I saw my boyfriend sitting on the warm, comfy couch, and I just lost it. All sensibility, rational thinking, and composure was left spilling down the city streets alongside my many tears.

I fell apart onto the hard, wooden floors.

In a panic, my boyfriend called my mom and asked what to do. My mom suggested that he convince me to take a shower and allow me to calm down. After much screaming back and forth, he persuaded me.

I dragged my cold, shaking body into the warm shower. I cried while lying in the tub as the warm water from the shower flooded over me. From that day forward, I hated the rain.

Humans are not creatures who naturally relish in discomfort. We make most of the decisions in our life as a means to actually create more safety, more comfort, and by any means possible, avoid the rain, the mud, the cold, and the essential death of self. But perhaps, this is the very invitation we so desperately need. Perhaps it's true that "in filth it will be found." What if your calling, purpose, and anointing is connected to the very things your flesh wants to avoid.

In the New Testament, the word translated as "grace" is the Greek word *charis*, for which Strong's Concordance gives this definition: "Graciousness (as gratifying), of manner or act ; especially the divine influence upon the heart, and its reflection in the life; including gratitude)."

Spiritual gifts or *charismata*, which come from the word family *charis*, is defined in the New Bible Dictionary as "grace coming to visible effect in word or deed." A Greek word that is related to *charis* is *charisma*, or gracious gift. The spiritual gifts that are offered to us through the filling of the Holy Spirit is God's divine influence upon the heart being made visible!

GOD'S FREE GIFTS

The grace that God has given us is a free gift. It is the empowerment to do the things He has created for us to do from the beginning of time! Don't allow anything to stop you from cashing in that gift card.

*F*AITHFULNESS AND OBEDIENCE ARE THE KEYS TO GROWING INTO THE THINGS GOD HAS FOR US.

When the Holy Spirit came upon those first believers at Pentecost, they suddenly had all the power they needed to follow Christ, even unto death, if needed. Even the disciples fell short in their own strength. Yet while Jesus was on earth, He promised us that He would send the Spirit. Jesus says in John 14:26 (NIV), *"But the Advocate, the Holy Spirit, whom the Father will send in my name, will teach you all things and will remind you of everything I have said to you."*

Through the power of the Holy Spirit, we can become transformed from the inside out. After being baptized in the Holy Spirit, Peter preached with power:

> *Peter's words pierced their hearts, and they said to him and to the other apostles, "Brothers, what should we do?" Peter replied, "Each of you must repent of your sins and turn to God, and be baptized in the name of Jesus Christ for the forgiveness of your sins. Then you will receive the gift of the Holy Spirit. This*

promise is to you, to your children, and to those far away—all
who have been called by the Lord our God."

(Acts 2:37-39 NLT)

The same Peter who denied Jesus, now spoke with boldness and led thousands into repentance and salvation through Jesus. It is impossible to be Spirit-filled and live apathetically. There is an overflow that comes as you allow the Holy Spirit to consume you. Your "dry season" is over. According to Scripture, the dry season is a lie. Don't take the bait! Jesus says that you shall live in *overflow*. John 7:37-39 (NIV) says:

On the last and greatest day of the festival, Jesus stood and
said in a loud voice, "Let anyone who is thirsty come to me and
drink. Whoever believes in me, as Scripture has said, rivers of
***living water will flow from within them."** By this he meant the*
Spirit, whom those who believed in him were later to receive.
Up to that time the Spirit had not been given, since Jesus had
not yet been glorified.

This is the life God has for you, a life of overflow. God wants to fill us with His Holy Spirit to saturate our churches with His glory and for it to spill out into every area of life. Every area! Nothing is off limits, and God does not desire to be contained to our Sunday schedules and the compartments into which we put "holy" things.

Ezekiel 36:25-29 (NIV) says:

I will sprinkle clean water on you, and you will be clean; I will
cleanse you from all your impurities and from all your idols. I
will give you a new heart and put a new spirit in you; I will

remove from you your heart of stone and give you a heart of flesh. And I will put my Spirit in you and move you to follow my decrees and be careful to keep my laws. Then you will live in the land I gave your ancestors; **you will be my people, and I will be your God.** *I will save you from all your uncleanness. I will call for the grain and make it plentiful and will not bring famine upon you.*

The fourth wave that is coming will lead to national repentance. It is a confrontation therapy, if you will. The Holy God we worship and follow wants to cleanse us from the inside out. According to Ezekiel, He desires to put a *new* heart and *new* Spirit in us. For us to possess the land, we need a new Spirit. We need to be born again and be saved from all of our uncleanliness. According to Romans 6, we need to go all in and become unbound from the world and be bound to Christ.

RIPPLE EFFECT REVIVAL

The prophetic showdown will ignite repentance on a massive scale. Every time I close my eyes and think about this revival wave that is coming, I am consumed by the hope of the saints baptizing and praying for people in parks and on streets across the nation. Every revival creates a ripple. I refer to this move of God as the "ripple effect revival" because I believe the impact God is making on individuals is multiplying, accelerating, and pulsating outward. Just like throwing a large stone into a lake, the waters surrounding are impacted—much like those who come into contact with a truly revived, on-fire, burning believer for Jesus.

When Christians are revived, we live differently. There is evidence of our "revivedness," so to speak. Our homes become ordered and places of peace. Our families become reconciled and marriages become intimate and restored. The people are gripped at the preaching of the Gospel, and generosity is no longer a twisting of the arm—we re-budget our finances around how to give more instead of excuses to give less.

GOD IS CONFRONTING US.

The life of a revived Christian should provoke jealousy in the unbeliever. Joy in every season, peace in every storm, and community that stirs one another on and loves each other in all things and despite all things.

God has heard our prayers for revival in the land, and He is confronting us with water. The problem with baptisms is they require a response. You're either wet or you're dry. I encourage you not to go back and forth about whether you should be baptized again. Rather, invite the Holy Spirit to search you. Are you *saturated* with His love, or has your heart grown dull and dry.

Sand appears on the shore as the ocean waves crash onto the coastline and break them down. Allow the Holy Spirit to break up the fallow ground. Allow Him to go deep in and cleanse you. Allow the baptism waters to shock your nervous system and awaken you once again. Then go, and baptize others in the name of the Father, Son, and Holy Spirit.

12

The Fifth Wave— Cleaning House

We need revival because we need to be reawakened and reconnected—without it, we are essentially non-essential in culture and society. I am not talking about becoming more "culturally relevant" to fill more seats in a room, I mean having real God solutions to a culture in chaos. Revival reestablishes the link between us and God. Now, of course, sure, you can reconnect to God in your warm, cozy bed with a cup of fine tea, but the reality is, many of us need to become shaken before we can be poured out. We need to be moved before we birth movements. This isn't poetry—its historical evidence based on years of Christian history of our apathy and worldly distraction lulling us to sleep while a remnant of believers pays the price, leads revival, and saves the nations from destruction.

WHAT DO YOU SEE?

I begin this chapter with a really simple exercise. I'd like you to take out a piece of paper and a pen and jot down a few things. I want you to think of the house or the apartment that is three doors away from you. Now, write down in detail as many things you can about the home, the décor, the surroundings.

Now think of a house or apartment that is ten doors away from you. Write down the details of the place, what it looks like, the décor, and surroundings.

Here is a little bonus exercise. I want you to write down in great detail the people who live in those two homes. What are their names? Where do they work? What needs do they have? How are they doing emotionally and/or spiritually right now?

Okay…did you finish the exercise?

I urge you not to continue reading and just filling your mind with more knowledge without pausing to engage in what I'm writing about.

If you completed the exercise, a majority (including me!) will have pretty empty pages—unless we glanced out our window or down the hallway! We read books on revival, we attend Sunday church services, and we even level up our faith by fasting and praying together for revival. Yet, we have missed the simple things.

EYES TO SEE

Jesus tells us to love our neighbors, but we are so consumed by doing our form of religion that we don't have eyes to see. We aren't paying attention to what's actually happening around us. Social media is burdening us to be empathetic toward people we will never meet—and for many of us, this burden is too great to bear. For some of us, the people on our own street are hurting, dying, and living a life without God—yet we are sharing social media posts that feel like justice and patting ourselves on the back for how good we are. This current everyday pattern is disturbing and robbing you from your calling. Period. The fires of revival fall on crucified lives with eyes lifted high.

We can read in the Bible that the last days look very much like *these* days.

So what hope do we have?

The apostle Paul writes to Timothy, his mentee:

> **You, however,** *know all about my teaching, my way of life, my purpose, faith, patience, love, endurance, persecutions, sufferings—what kinds of things happened to me in Antioch, Iconium and Lystra, the persecutions I endured.* **Yet the Lord rescued me** *from all of them. In fact, everyone who wants to live a godly life in Christ Jesus will be persecuted, while evildoers and impostors will go from bad to worse, deceiving and being deceived. But as for you, continue in what you have learned and have become convinced of, because you know those from whom you learned it.*
>
> (2 Timothy 3:10-14 NIV)

No matter what the years 2020, 2021, 2022, 2023, 2024, 2050, 2100, 3000 look like…

+ *You, however,* know God.

- *You, however,* serve God.

- As Christians, we are not thrown about by every cultural storm—we remember that God *will rescue us* from those who do evil.

We get to be part of His mission here on earth. The privilege is overwhelming when you think about it. It's heartbreaking that even for a moment—or for some of us, years—we have allowed the enemy to rob us of such an incredible opportunity.

The power, the miracles, the signs and wonders are on the streets and backing those who will preach the Gospel! We are launching a training center because God is raising up a remnant that can no longer be watchers—they are saying, "Here I am Lord, send me! Whatever the cost, I'll pay it."

"*H*ERE I AM LORD, SEND ME! WHATEVER THE COST, I'LL PAY IT."

Jesus invited His very first disciples to leave the ordinary and to *come and see* (John 1:39 NLT). We need to be taught how to study the Word of God, have accurate theology, and then be taught how to *do* what we read about. The word *see* in the original Greek is the word *horaó*, which actually means "behold, perceive, see" or properly, "to stare at, to discern clearly (physically or mentally); by extension, to attend to; *to experience*" (Strong's G3708).

I've heard some tired, frustrated preachers proclaim from the pulpit, "Christianity isn't about an experience." Yet when I study the New Testament, I am confronted by the constant need for the experience of something supernatural. Jesus didn't hold back when it came to providing His followers with a supernatural, Kingdom-life experience. What we see in the New Testament is what revival looks like, feels like, and sounds like.

SOMETHING DIFFERENT

When we begin to experience a new way of life, we will invite others into that life. Not every event that we do with *Saturate Global* is revival. I have discussed with Parker and our team that I'm looking for a certain *je ne sais quoi* that happens when hungry, humble, desperate souls come into heavy, tangible *glory* where the Holy Spirit searches the deep things in us and calls us *higher*.

Revival is more than a Christian conference, and it's not just a big event with excited people.

It is the Church, the saints, being awakened, revived, and set ablaze with the Kingdom of God. It's when the fallow ground of our hearts is broken up, and we become reawakened to our first love. We rediscover the treasure in the field, the pearl of great value! The illusion from the lures of fame, fortune, and comfort lose their luster and we become obsessed with one thing—knowing Christ and making Him known to others.

REVIVAL IS MORE THAN A CHRISTIAN CONFERENCE.

I believe that God is cleaning His house. The bride of Christ is being purified and returning to her first love. Many people are praying for a billon-soul harvest, but we need the storehouses to be renovated first.

Around the globe, we have a problem in the Church that has become a roadblock to revival. Scripture tells us, *"You shall have no other gods before me"* (Deuteronomy 5:7 NIV). You may not find yourself visiting temples of other gods or praying to a statue of Buddha, but we can turn the love of money, relationships, career, comfort, even success in ministry, and "being a good Christian" into an idol.

There is a dangerous temptation to take the Jesus of the Bible and twist Him into a version of Jesus we are more comfortable with.

Could Jesus possibly ask you in the next six months to sell all of your belongings and give them to the poor? To pick up your mat and walk out your healing? To go two by two into the city nearby and cast out demons in His name? Yeah, He could, and He probably is, to some degree.

13

All In

September 20, 2017. I was in labor with our second son, Ethan. For the previous nine months, I had a mostly normal pregnancy, minus the constant nausea and vomit. Around 10:30 p.m., my water broke and we rushed to the hospital in Newport where I would be delivering our son. After a few hours of contractions, I was now in the "window" to get an epidural. The anesthesiologist came in and had me sit still on the edge of the hospital bed. In between painful contractions, the epidural was administered, which would give me a few hours of relief from the pain and allow me to rest a bit and prepare to push the baby out.

Alongside Parker, two of the girls I discipled were in the delivery room with me. As we chatted, I noticed that the contractions were increasing in severity. We quickly called in the nurse, and they gave me another "dose" of pain medication through the epidural. After about thirty minutes, I noticed something unusual. Half my body was experiencing extreme pain with each contraction, and the other half of my body was mostly numb. We called in another nurse to find out that only half of the epidural was administered correctly.

As my labor continued, half of my body was completely engaged in every contraction, pressure pain, and transition of labor. The other half of my body was immobile, unable to engage in labor, and left me feeling helpless, weak, and defeated. I screamed at the nurse to figure out a solution while sweat dripped down my face and my body was shaking and unable to bear down during transition. The truth is, it would have been far better to have had a completely natural childbirth than the pain and agony of a half-engaged body. Ethan arrived a few hours later, a healthy little boy. As I held him in my arms, a Kingdom revelation filled my mind.

The Bible says in Revelation 3:15-20 (NIV):

> *I know your deeds, that you are neither cold nor hot. I wish you were either one or the other! So, because you are lukewarm—neither hot nor cold—I am about to spit you out of my mouth. …Those whom I love I rebuke and discipline. So be earnest and repent. Here I am! I stand at the door and knock. If anyone hears my voice and opens the door, I will come in and eat with that person, and they with me.*

God wants us to be fully engaged in what He is doing. How often have we settled for a lukewarm version of our faith, believing that the King of kings gave us His Holy Spirit for us to be so preoccupied by so many things in life that simply do not matter. We are tossed all over the place when it comes to spiritual warfare, unaware of how the Kingdom and authority work. We watch friends, tormented, paying for one counseling session after another, unable to offer them freedom and unaware of how to cast a demon out—or even worse, believing that we can't! Spiritual disciplines such as fasting and solitude have been marked as legalistic, as we have become over-obsessed with self-care and personality tests.

In early December 2017, I heard the Lord whisper to me, "You need to be ALL IN." I believed this was a word for my husband, Parker, as he spent his days working at Equinox as a personal trainer, while pioneering a micro church planting movement and raising our two babies under two years old. We prayed together late into the evening and decided that he should transition into full-time ministry. Parker began support raising and our churches entered into a new season of health, vision, and expansion. Yet, it seemed like something was missing.

As mid-January rolled around, I had all of my strategies in place to expand my business (a successful creative agency for luxury brands called NYC-Collective), lead Salt Churches alongside Parker, and oversee outreach efforts. My desire was to be a hard-working successful entrepreneur, supportive wife, and a good mother to our 18-month-old son David and our 6-month-old cuddly baby bear Ethan.

I could easily *do it all*. I was the queen of multitasking, extremely resourceful, and highly favored in the fashion industry. I had attended conferences about marketplace ministry and believed that the open doors and favor so clearly outlined that my ministry position was in the fashion industry. As I boarded the plane with my family, heading to New York for a rare preaching opportunity (rare in the sense that I wasn't being invited to preach anywhere, ha!), the Holy Spirit whispered again, "YOU need to be ALL IN."

I wrestled in my economy seat, with Ethan drooling on my sweaty arm and reworked my message that was for "everyone else." What did God want me to speak to these students? They need to be all in! Got it. Most often, I believe it is hard for a preacher to realize that the words God whispers aren't always for everyone else. Sometimes they are for the preacher! We have all heard the preachers encourage the congregation with an appeal and everyone is thinking, *Homeboy, that revelation is for you!*

You NEED TO BE ALL IN.

I decided to take out my journal and asked God if there were areas where I had compartmentalized my life. I had reached many people with the Gospel through my business, created income for several other believers in our church, and my company had given our family the flexibility to move across the country without any savings to start church planting. This was obviously God's will for my life, based on the favor, success, and fruit. Can I be completely honest with you, and share one of the greatest kingdom secrets I have discovered over the last few years. Favor, fruit, and family are all great signposts that you are on the right track, but at the end of the day you need to sometimes pause and ask the Lord, "Am I still doing what You want me to be doing?"

Following Jesus, discovering your identity, and walking out your calling cannot simply be relegated to five steps you read in a book or what someone prayed over you during an importation service. This is all about intimacy. It's about allowing God to search deeper, calling you higher.

BREAD CRUMB TRAILS

Throughout the week, I was haunted by confirmations that I was readily trying to ignore. Isn't it hilarious that we all do this. We pray and ask God to speak to us, to show us what to do, to lead us into taking the next steps. Then when it doesn't fit within the box of expectations we have put the Lord of the universe in, we dismiss it, discount it, or wait for thousands of confirmations before we will act. Some of y'all (I can say y'all now because I live in North Carolina!) are sitting on a prophetic word that has been confirmed—and you are praying and hoping that the Lord will change His mind. I pray this is the sign you have been waiting for, it is time to step out and act on the things the Lord is speaking to you about.

SOMETHING DIFFERENT

I sat on my mother's bed crying, wrestling with what God was speaking to me. In the background, on my mother's bedroom television, Joyce Meyer was sharing about her transition from being successful at sales and God asking her to quit her job to study the Word of God and preach. I'll be honest, the message playing in the background felt "weirdly" relatable. Joyce shared about living by faith when God asks you to do something new; and that although it may be hard, it's worth it.

Now don't get me wrong, I believe with every fiber of my being that God *desires* His people to be in the marketplace. I have been part of His transforming power in board meetings, at high-profile events, and during client photo shoots. Every believer of Jesus, full of the Holy

Spirit, is a saint. The saints get to do the work of the ministry. One of my greatest passions is to activate people of influence in the spheres they are in for His glory and the expansion of the Kingdom of God here on earth.

However, if God is telling us to do something different or new, don't become disobedient in your *diligence to a former season*. As I continued to pray and seek wisdom from advisors, God told me to give away my business. This was very difficult for me mentally. It made much more sense to sell my successful company to continue to provide income for my family. Why would I give it away?

One thing I have learned over the past thirteen years about following Jesus with all of my heart, is this—Jesus is worth obeying, and His way of doing something is not always the same as your way of doing something.

Jesus not only forgave my sins when I screamed out to Him, broken, and clamoring for peace, Jesus is also the Lord of my life, and I am committed to following Him no matter the cost. People often comment how radically obedient Parker and I are, but the truth is, there is no other way any of us should live. Jesus is always inviting us into an exchange, and the temptation lies in thinking we are giving God more than He is giving us. We sell everything we own to purchase the field, knowing that there is a treasure in it, and the lie is found as we focus on what the field cost us, not what the field has in it. (See Matthew 13:44-46.)

NYC-Collective was a gift of resource in the form of a seed that looked like starting a business. God had given me the idea, the open doors, and the clients, and I am thankful for that season. Yet, if I was honest, for the first year and half we were in California, I had been living half engaged in what God was asking me to now birth. God was speaking to me about revival, and I was stuck in a past season.

BREAKING THE CHAINS OF RELIGION

Since 2016, God has shown me that I will never be a pastor. My job title will never give me access to the conference speaking circuit. The Lord told me, "It won't be your title, but the evidence of fruit that will open doors for you to preach all around the earth." I'll be honest, I was relieved. I struggle emotionally with the "networking" in the Green Rooms and feel exhausted trying to position myself in the celebrity Christian manufactured world. I feel like a square peg in a round hole, and the cry of John the Baptist permeates me. Sometimes I really understand why he chose the wilderness over the temple.

Jesus has asked me to go "ALL IN" as a full-time missionary in one of the spiritually neediest places in the world—the United States of America. I lie in bed awake through the night, praying and petitioning for the spiritually dead in the land of the free. God has called me to wake up a sleeping church and to break the chains of religion. I believe a big part of my calling is to lead Christians to Christ and equip them to lift up their eyes and expand the Kingdom of God wherever they are, inviting them to a banquet where there is always more available.

I am obsessed with Jesus and believe that *now* is the time for a *revival* through repentance sustained by discipleship in new era churches that look like training centers.

The Church must be activating the saints to share the Gospel. We need a Gospel of power, not just merely good ideas. Following Jesus often looks like following a bread-crumb trail. One step, one vision, one simple obedience at a time.

14

The Sixth Wave—Exposure

SMOKE AND MIRRORS

I am aware that many people reading this book have likely never stepped into a nightclub. That's fine. Nightclubs create a space for people to feel…something. It's a place to forget Monday and become alive for a few hours, dancing to the bass of the DJ, while a promoter fills spilled glasses with vodka and cranberry juice and the disco ball reflects the little thousand lights in the curated, blacked out room.

Immediate value is placed on those sitting atop leather banquettes—and for a young twenty-year-old girl, the gratification of being seen, known, and temporarily loved is, well, addictive. The industry is much like a drug, to which I was not only an addict but a dealer.

I worked in the nightclub industry for seven years, which basically is like getting a PhD in the industry, which ages out most people at around twenty-five years old. I personally knew the doormen of the top clubs in Miami and in New York City. I understood the nuance of the impossible VIP list and what qualifies an eager Wall Street trader the ability to enter or not. Nightclubs create an illusion that you can be anything, if you know the right anyone.

I was working for one of the top nightclub groups in Manhattan, which required long hours in the office creating VIP lists and late nights in short skirts and fur jackets, freezing outside with a clipboard in hand repeating verbatim, "Did you purchase a table? Who are you here with?" About halfway through my shift, I would head into the abyss of sparkles, patron shots, and sip a Diet Coke and vodka (also known as a skinny b*tch), and dance as goofy as possible (known in my group as "bad dancing"), while drawing as much attention to ourselves and our group of Manhattan elites as possible. Often, in my leather clutch, I'd have with my face paint, and my friends and I would paint the faces of those at our table with tribal marks that identified our group apart from everyone else. Everyone wanted the face paint, everyone wanted to be on the inside of the inside.

1 A.M. VERSUS 1 P.M.

Nightclubs are full of layers, and for the average person, once they pay the high cost for access, they only discover that they are still on the outside. They are now given permission to purchase $21 drinks and watch the real fun happen, on the inside of the VIP area, which requires more status or finances for access.

Heading into New Year's Eve season, I had to visit one of the more popular clubs to outline the room for ticket sales and estimate how many tables we could fit in for the popular annual event.

I'll let you in on a big industry secret: one o'clock in the *afternoon* in a nightclub is very different from one o'clock in the *morning*.

The bar manager unlocked the door and let me in. There was no doorman, no line, no crowds, no lights, no confetti, no bass, no drinks, no sparkle. Just filthy sticky floors, bare walls desperately needing attention, and the smell of stale beer wafting through the cold, still, stale room.

I sat down on sticky maroon leather and placed my notebook on the rigid metal table in front of me. I didn't know why, but tears slowly started to trickle down my cheeks. With each blink, dripped burning salt water, my soul overflowing out of my heavy lined eyelids. I realized, in that moment, everything in my life was *nothing but smoke and mirrors.* Anyone can throw a sparkly dress on a sticky-floor spirit.

Mark 8:36 (NLT) says, *"And what do you benefit if you gain the whole world but lose your own soul?"*

There are many of us who are within the four walls of a church and still living a life of smoke and mirrors.

> The Christian life is one of paradox, caught in the assurance of God's ever-presence and a constant stroke of varying vulnerability. We want to believe; we want to surrender; we want to love; we want to unpack ourselves and put on the whole armor of God. "Yes, I know one doesn't even want to be cured of one's pride," Lewis says, as we return to his 1954 letter, "because it gives pleasure. But the pleasure of pride is like the pleasure of scratching. If there is an itch one does want to scratch; but it is much nicer to have neither the itch nor the scratch. As long as we have the itch of self-regard, we shall want the pleasure of self-approval: but the happiest moments are those when we forget our precious selves and have neither, but have everything else (God, our fellow-humans, animals, the garden & the sky) instead.[1]

I believe that the sixth wave coming to America is the kindness of the Lord, turning on the lights in the dark, overcrowded nightclub of the soul. I think for many of us, God is giving the opportunity to repent while we can. What may be very jolting for many in the body of Christ will be what is revealed at the "1 p.m. hour" when the lights are turned on and the sticky floors in us and around us are on display. My prayer is that now, we do the deep work of the soul. I pray, by the power of the Holy Spirit, that we can be spared this exposure, and when the light shines, a pure spotless bride will be revealed.

GOD IS GIVING THE OPPORTUNITY TO REPENT WHILE WE CAN.

The letter Paul wrote to the church in Corinth, rings like an alarm clock on our nightstands today:

I am jealous for you with a godly jealousy. I promised you to one husband, to Christ, so that I might present you as a pure virgin to him. But I am afraid that just as Eve was deceived by the serpent's cunning, your minds may somehow be led astray from your sincere and pure devotion to Christ. For if someone comes to you and preaches a Jesus other than the Jesus we preached, or if you receive a different spirit from the Spirit you received, or a different gospel from the one you accepted, you put up with it easily enough.

(2 Corinthians 11:1-4 NIV)

Oh, how we have strayed from the true Gospel. Forgive us, God. Heal our hearts, cleanse our minds, and stir within us a conviction to stand for the truth by the power of Your love.

THE TRUE GOSPEL

We so long for any Gospel that allows us to protect our own mind, will, and emotions. Yet the true Gospel is one of surrender, one of laying down our life, one of losing our life to gain His instead. We believe that God, who created the universe, who breathed us into being, who sent His Son, Jesus, to die for us so that we may be reconciled to Him; we believe that this almighty God is satisfied with religious duty and not a cut and consecrated heart.

Charles Spurgeon wrote:

It is a sorrowful fact that many who are spiritually alive greatly need reviving. It is sorrowful because it is a proof of the existence of much spiritual evil. A man in sound health with every part of his body in a vigorous condition does not

— 137 —

need reviving. He requires daily sustenance, but reviving would be quite out of place. If he has not yet attained maturity growth will be most desirable, but a hale hearty young man wants no reviving, it would be thrown away upon him. Who thinks of reviving the noonday sun, the ocean at its flood, or the year at its prime? The tree planted by the rivers of water loaded with fruit needs not excite our anxiety for its revival, for its fruitfulness and beauty charm everyone. Such should be the constant condition of the sons of God. Feeding and lying down in green pastures and led by the still waters they ought not always to be crying, "my leanness, my leanness, woe unto me."[2]

Right now, I pray for you, dear reader. I thank you for the providential opportunity to repent and bear open your heart to Him. I pray for all the ways you may have been deceived to be exposed to you RIGHT NOW through the power of the Holy Spirit. I ask that the Spirit of Revelation would come now, and bring you up HIGHER. Search us, Oh God!

Write here (yes, right in this book):

What do you need to repent of?

_____

_____

_____

_____

What needs to be given to the Lord?

What has become an idol?

What will not make it through the refiner's fire?

Endnotes

1. C.S. Lewis, "Lewis on Love," *The Four Loves*; posted February 13, 2019 by Zach Kincaid; https://www.cslewis.com/lewis-on-love; accessed August 17, 2022.

2. C.H. Spurgeon, "What Is a Revival?"; *The Spurgeon Archive, Sword and Trowel*, December 1866; https://archive.spurgeon.org/s_and_t/wir1866.php; accessed August 17, 2022.

15

You May Be Too Busy for Revival

When my husband and I watched the *Batman* trilogy, my spirit felt stirred and provoked. There is a scene in *Dark Knight Rises* where the power has been given back to "The People." In this scene, people are being brought into court for their crimes against society. The judge on the seat gives the people the choice of how justice will be served. The criminal is not given a fair trial and has two options: either walk the ice and face a cold and morbid death, or be killed immediately on the spot.

What I saw in *Dark Knight Rises* is so much like what we saw on the news in 2020. While watching the riots and witnessing complete anarchy on the streets, I wondered to myself, *Can this really be happening? Where has the bold Church gone?*

I believe the lesson God is taking us all through, is to see if we will desire God and seek Him and His ways *above all else*. Will believers go into the secret place while the world is pounding on our doors for a public statement on race, homosexuality, politics, scandal, and more? Where does our response come from? Where does our hope come from? Do we hope and believe, despite all we see and hear?

The word I heard God say the month before we launched the first weekend of Saturate in 2020 was, "If salt loses its saltiness, it's no longer of any use." Many of us know this Scripture verse in Matthew 5:13, and yet those words haunted me in a fresh and powerful way, which is what revelation does!

WHAT HAS HAPPENED TO US?

I cried out on my cold, wooden prayer room floor, "Lord, please protect us and please help us lead in whatever it is You are doing." Despite the demonic agenda of Covid, perhaps God was using the global pandemic to reveal what was in the hearts and minds of the leaders of many churches. Have we lost our saltiness? Have we become nonessential? Did the entire season reveal the many idols we had and have put on center stage?

Here is a harsh reality—you are likely too busy for revival. Or better said, you may be too distracted for revival.

What has happened to us? Have our hearts grown dull?

Author and speaker Jordan B. Peterson writes in his book *Beyond Order*, "It can be overwhelming to open ourselves up to the beauty in the world that we as adults have painted over with simplicity. In not doing so, however—in not taking a proper walk with a young child, for example—we lose track of the grandeur and the awe the untrammeled world is constantly capable of producing and reduce our lives to bleak necessity."[1]

What if God invited you to be a small part of revival, but it was in the city you hate the most? If you're a minister, what if revival was going to happen in your church on the weekend you're out of town, or the church next door? What if the big media platform you built is meant to be handed over to someone else?

I receive hundreds of emails from people who believe revival is going to happen in their church and/or city. I believe that is a great start, because you can't have revival without faith, but what is next? So few people understand that revival requires sacrifice. It requires us to lay down our plans. It requires us to go where He is going, to do what He is doing. Many of us are merely surviving, distracted, and allowing the culture to tell us where to extend our emotional energy, where to sow our finances, and where to place our trust.

REVIVAL REQUIRES SACRIFICE.

DON'T MISS IT

If you're really brutally honest, how much of your budget is set aside for you to have finances to *go* if God tells you to *go?* How much of your income are you sowing into ministries that are doing the work of revival? One of the most heart-wrenching experiences I had in 2020 was seeing a church orchestrate a prayer night for revival, but refused to grab a coffee to partner with us as thousands were being saved, healed, and set free right on their very shore, down the street from their church.

Is your work, routine, disciplines, ministry, personal budget, or wanderlust mentality an idol for you? Are you "ALL IN" only to find yourself "ALL OUT" once someone disagrees with you, when the culture becomes fierce and you lose friends, or when the world entangles you and perhaps you get a promotion at work that you just can't give up?

I'm writing all this to lay a framework as to why we have yet to see a sustained revival in the United States of America. The bait for comfort and distraction is low-hanging fruit, and unless we are continually provoked and the flames of our souls stoked, we will yet again be another generation telling stories of what "God once did." I pray it isn't so.

SOMETHING MORE THAN EXCITEMENT.

I simply *refuse* to have my best stories about God working in me through me, be behind me. I am inviting you to open your calendar and begin to prioritize revival.

I dare you to risk it all and create space for Him to move. Ask the Lord to reveal to you those who are burning on fire for Jesus, and have the evidence of the fire in their lives. Go and see. Learn and serve ministries that are running in the promises of your life. I remember getting to a point in my walk with Jesus where I just couldn't continue on without seeing God's power in my life. I could no longer preach sermons about the power without demonstrating its effects. I felt desperate. I bought revival books on a discounted book reselling website and devoted myself to study what the Lord had done. I begged the Lord, "Set me on fire, use me!" I prayed for people on the street; and still to this day I find conferences and trainings where I can learn and glean from revival practitioners.

WE NEED MORE THAN JUST EXCITEMENT AND ENTHUSIASM.

We need more than just excitement and enthusiasm. Thousands of youth fill stadiums every year, and yet we see suicide and depression rates climbing. I fully believe that we need more passion in our pulpits, more conviction, and a return to preaching about the Spirit-filled life. I believe that God is raising up a remnant that is devoted to the Word and can move in miracles, signs, and wonders. I believe that revival wildfires will spread as we teach people how to dwell in the presence of the Most High God and stay burning as they learn how to follow the Holy Spirit. I pray that we would not settle for great revelation, but we would press in, ascend higher, and pursue a life that makes the world wonder.

Charles Spurgeon writes:

> If they hear the Word of God they are never stirred by it; enthusiasm is an unknown luxury. ...Vital godliness is not revived in Christians by mere excitement, by crowded meetings, by the stamping of the foot, or the knocking of the pulpit cushion, or the delirious bawlings of ignorant zeal; these are the stock in trade of revivals among dead souls, but to revive living saints other means are needed. Intense excitement may produce a revival of the animal, but how can it operate upon the spiritual, for the spiritual demands other food than that which stews in the fleshpots of mere carnal enthusiasm. The Holy Ghost must come into the living heart through living truth, and so bring nutriment and stimulant to the pining spirit, for so only can it be revived. This, then, leads us to the conclusion that if we are to obtain a revival we must go directly to the Holy Ghost for it, and not resort to the machinery of the professional revival-maker. The true vital spark of heavenly flame comes from the Holy Ghost, and the priests of the Lord must beware of strange fire. There is no spiritual vitality in anything except as the Holy Spirit is all in all in the work; and if our vitality has fallen near to zero, we can only have it renewed by him who first kindled it in us. We must go to the cross and look up to the dying Savior, and expect that the Holy Spirit will renew our faith and quicken all our graces. We must feed anew by

faith upon the flesh and blood of the Lord Jesus, and so the Holy Ghost will recruit our strength and give us a revival.[2]

Endnotes

1. Jordan B. Peterson, *Beyond Order: 12 More Rules for Life* (New York: Penguin Random House, 2021).

2. C.H. Spurgeon, "What Is a Revival?" *The Spurgeon Archive, Sword and Trowel*; December 1866; https://archive.spurgeon.org/s_and_t/wir1866.php; accessed August 17, 2022.

16

My Revival Mistake

Revivalist Leonard Ravenhill (1907-1994) wrote, "Prayer is no substitute for work; equally true is it that work is no substitute for prayer." If we want to see revival, we need people of prayer.

Did you know that there has never been a revival without prevailing prayer first?

As I write this chapter and finish writing this book, I am processing what the Lord is doing through the ministry my husband and I lead. After God highlighted to us in 2021 the "wells of revival," specifically from the First and Second Great Awakenings, we had moved out of our home and into a renovated trailer with our family of five to host revival events in fields across the country. God moved powerfully in Philadelphia, Kentucky, and North Carolina. Our team and several hundred volunteers helped us set up stages, pitch up tents, and organize our first ever camp meeting based on a vision I had while filming at Sid Roth's studio.[1] There were many miracles that took place during the summer of 2021, as we trained thousands to cast out demons and share the Gospel.

God took us on an adventure that summer that ultimately led us just north of Wilmington, North Carolina. We sensed God's presence was really strong in the area, and God was helping us establish a base for our ministry, a refuge for our family, and a place to train and send missionaries to America.

As our team moved from across the country, we gathered in my new home for prayer meetings on our back deck and made plans and organized for the following summer. As we began to plan for Summer 2022, and the National Camp Meeting, we had been invited to preach over Easter weekend at Global River, a local church in Wilmington. During the Easter weekend, unexpectantly, revival began to break out and we baptized eighty people over the weekend.

People cried out in repentance and the lead pastor said with humble sincerity, "We will do whatever it takes to host this." They invested more than $10,000 to prepare their beautiful property for weekly revival nights, and our team was excited to jump back into the war of winning souls!

Earlier that year, we had won on an auction a 100' x 140' event tent (for only $168!) and were thrilled to finally set it up along with thirty hungry volunteers. The first Friday night, we witnessed many people give their lives to Jesus and several healings take place. We continued meeting on Friday nights, working hard to orchestrate brand-new volunteers, order signage, organize a prayer and ministry team, find worship leaders, and preach the Gospel! Each Friday that we met, we saw between twenty-five to thirty people baptized, many salvations, many healings and deliverances.

After about the seventh week of gathering, I noticed the same people coming. People were no longer reaching their lost friends and neighbors, and the ministry time was becoming more and more self-focused. There seemed to be a resistance in the spirit, and our team was becoming tired and losing enthusiasm. During this time, we were also receiving several prophetic words from trusted prophets that we needed to purchase our own land and establish a place to train and send others.

With only a month till the National Camp Meeting, and more than 2,000 people registered, we began raising funds and searching for land in the region. In the matter of three weeks, we miraculously raised $400,000, but was still short to make an offer on any land that would fit our needs. With only two weeks until the big event, we halted the Friday night meetings and began to frantically prepare for the incoming group. Logistics became insanity, as we found a beautiful property to rent nearby—another God miracle!—and had to break down, set up, hire a stage, order thirty portable potties, pick cactus out of the ground, set up lighting for one hundred camp sites, order generators, and more! In the swirl of planning and preparing, the concentrated, focused, fervent prayer was put to the side.

This was a grave mistake.

Over the four days, we saw hundreds of people repent, be baptized, get healed, and more, yet the entire weekend just felt "off" to me. Prevailing prayer was missing—the cutting of the heart that can't come from wise and persuasive words. The magnitude of the ripple that comes from real revival when people turn away from their lives and go into the deep end of their faith. While we have received testimonies of a handful of people who were marked and have continued to go on and share the Gospel and baptize others, we were missing the wide sweeping move of the Holy Spirit that changes regions, that transforms nations.

It's a mistake I will never repeat.

As I finish editing this book, our team is preparing for our first-ever "Gospel Raid" in New York City. With a vision to train 1,000 people over two days and then saturate the streets of Manhattan with the Gospel, we need hungry and humble servants of the Lord and a powerful move of the Spirit. In preparation, we have a daily prayer call at 9 a.m. each morning, and a week of prayer and fasting.

I have signed up myself and the Saturate Team for prayer trainings to learn from other intercession, and we have invited Mando Matthews, who leads Ekballo, to lead a prayer strike the night before. The intercession and prayer cannot be relegated to another team member, but I have found that the revivalist that God has called to lead but devote themselves to prayer, with the Holy Spirit as the lead intercessor (see Romans 8).

WHAT EXACTLY IS REVIVAL PRAYER?

The simplest explanation—prayer is taking time to talk to God. It is a direct address to the King of kings. Prayer is powerful and it is a privilege to have access to God. God hears our prayers, so we should engage in prayer as often as possible. Author Bob Sorge wrote:

> There are many things God has purposed for this planet, and they will most certainly happen; the only question is, will they happen in and with and through us? Will we participate? If we don't pray, God's purposes will happen, but they will not happen sooner. They will be delayed.
>
> See here the infinite power of God to accelerate things on earth and bring world events to their culmination. He can wrap this whole thing up whenever He wants to, but He's looking for a generation that refuses to be bypassed—a

generation that's so desperate to be included that they're giving themselves to incessant, violent prayer.

One of the most profound ways you can love someone is by praying for them. Intercession does something very powerful in the intercessor: It joins the heart of the intercessor to the heart of the one being prayed for. In intercession, you are investing yourself in another person's life. It's one of the secrets of the secret place. Our intercessory prayers thus become "cords of affection" which bind the hearts of believers to one another, joining the body of Christ together in the greatest of all virtues—love."[2]

There are so many incredible books on prayer by devout believers and authors such as E.M. Bounds, Bob Sorge, David Yonggi Cho, Rees Howells, Leonard Ravenhill, Lou Engle, Corey Russell, and Dutch Sheets. I would encourage you to read these books and learn the simple tools of praying and partnering with God through prayer. Prayer unites the body of believers in a way that no other "work" can.

American Christian pastor A.W. Tozer (1897-1963) highlights this truth when he wrote:

> Has it ever occurred to you that one hundred pianos all tuned to the same fork are automatically tuned to each other? They are of one accord by being tuned, not to each other, but to another standard to which each one must individually bow. So, one hundred worshipers met together, each one looking away to Christ, are in heart nearer to each other than they could possibly be, were they to become "unity" conscious and turn their eyes away from God to strive for closer fellowship.[3]

PRAYER WALKS

I encourage you when you finish this chapter, to set this book down and go on a prayer walk. This is a practice my husband and I have picked up that has drastically shifted our heart for our neighbors, our city, our state, and our nation.

Set a time, at least weekly and walk through your neighborhood, nearby park, mall, or wherever you feel led. Walk and pray. Ask the Lord to show you what He is doing in the area. Ask the Lord to highlight people to you and offer prayer to people as you go along.

Many of us know the popular salvation verse in Romans 10:9 (ESV), *"if you confess with your mouth that Jesus is Lord and believe in your heart that God raised him from the dead, you will be saved."*

But what does it actually mean for Jesus to be your Lord? I have often preached that many of us love and accept the free gift of forgiveness of our sins on the cross. We have reverence and appreciation to be given mercy in our darkest moments. The issue is, many of us are not following the *risen* Savior. Jesus is alive, this means that a response is required from us. When we confess that Jesus is our Lord, it means He is now in control. Is Jesus your Master, Ruler, in charge of your life?

Submission is so important if you want God to move. We pray for revival but struggle when God asks us to give freely of our finances, time, life. I believe that as we devote ourselves to prayer and fasting, it helps prepare us to be used by God. It removes the self-idolatry in our hearts and helps us refocus on what God is doing and our response. I believe that often the greatest moves of God come from a group of committed believers who have submitted their lives to God and pray together.

THE GREATEST MOVES OF GOD COME FROM A GROUP OF COMMITTED BELIEVERS WHO HAVE SUBMITTED THEIR LIVES TO GOD.

WHY STEWARDSHIP?

For a year, God told me to pick up pennies off the ground. It was the weirdest thing ever. Every time I saw a penny on the street, I would sense the Holy Spirit urging me to pick it up. Nowadays, pennies are basically worthless. They are annoying to carry around and you can't really purchase anything for a penny. After a little over a year, I was worshipping and I heard God say, "Do you know why I had you pick up pennies?" I quickly responded with, "Um, no." He then said to me, "I needed to trust you with pennies before I could trust you with lives."

You see, it was never really about pennies—it was about my heart and character before God. For years, I asked people to prophesy over my calling and gifting to preach, to reach people, etc. However, I often felt overlooked and unfulfilled in my calling, wondering when it would "happen." The truth is, *It* happens in the day-to-day, mundane moments.

Your calling to preach may start off with encouraging words to the person behind the counter. Your calling to lead a church may start with discipling one person. Your calling to see people healed starts with praying for people other than yourself. When it comes down to it, are you really aware of what God is doing around you? When you spend time with Jesus and follow Him, what do you naturally do? What are you passionate about? What problems do you want to fix? What is God highlighting to you in prayer?

I encourage you to ask God for a specific vision of what He is doing. Ask Him to show you. Keep persisting in prayer until He does. Then, step out in faith and believe that God is going to do what He spoke to you about. God is constantly testing our hearts. Do we really want the things we are praying for, or do we want an instant fix that makes us feel better about ourselves. In prayer, ask the Lord:

1. Why is revival important?

2. How can I learn more about revival?

3. What character traits in me need to be developed? Where am I lacking maturity?

4. Am I overflowing with the power of the Holy Spirit?

5. Where is God releasing revival right now, and how can I serve that?

Too often we can miss the very thing we were perhaps created for while looking at the fruit of years of stewardship and submission somewhere else. We can become so wrapped up in callings, passions, and giftings that we lose sight of why. When the sentence starts with "My," we lose the "Why."

The prayer that prevails must be fervent, earnest, and passionate. A modern translation of James 5:16 (NLT) reads: *"The earnest prayer of a righteous person has great power and produces wonderful results."* The emphasis is on the word, *"earnest."*

American revivalist Charles Finney (1792-1875) wrote:

> There are two kinds of means requisite to promote a revival of religion; the one to influence men, the other to influence God. The truth is employed to influence men, and prayer to move God.
>
> When I speak of moving God, I do not mean that God's mind is changed by prayer, or that His disposition or character is changed. But prayer produces such a change in us, as renders it consistent for God to do what would not be consistent for Him to do otherwise.
>
> When a sinner repents, that state of feeling makes it proper for God to forgive him. So when Christians, with the aid of the Holy Spirit, offer effectual prayer, their state of feeling render it proper for God to answer them. He was never unwilling to bestow the blessing on the condition that they felt right, and offered the right kind of prayer.
>
> Prayer is an essential link in the chain of causes that lead to a revival; as much so as truth is. Some have zealously used truth to convert men, and laid very little stress on prayer.

They have preached, and talked, and distributed tracts with great zeal, and then wondered that they had so little success. The reason was that they forgot to use the other branch of means—effectual prayer. They overlooked the fact, that truth by itself, will never produce the necessary effect without the Spirit of God.

Sometimes it happens that those who are the most engaged in employing truth are not the most engaged in prayer. This is unfortunate, for unless they—or some others—have the spirit of prayer, the truth, by itself, will do nothing but harden men in impenitence. Probably in the day of judgment it will be found that nothing is ever done by the truth, used ever so zealously, unless there is a spirit of prayer somewhere in connection with the presentation of truth.

Others err on the other side. Not that they lay too much stress on prayer, but they overlook the fact that prayer might be offered forever, by itself, and nothing would be done. Because sinners are not converted by direct contact with the Holy Ghost, but by the truth, employed as a means. To expect the conversion of sinners by prayer alone, without the employment of truth, is to tempt God.[4]

Endnotes

1. Sid Roth is host of the television program, *It's Supernatural!*

2. Bob Sorge, *Secrets of the Secret Place* (Oasis House, 2001).

3. A.W. Tozer, *The Pursuit of God: The Human Thirst for the Divine*; http://www.ntslibrary.com/PDF%20Books/Tozer_Pursuit_of_God.pdf; accessed August 17, 2022.

4. Charles Finney, ed. William Allen, *The Spiritual Preparation of a Soul Winner*, "How to Pray Effectually, Chapter I; https://www.charlesgfinney.com/finney-101/prepofswtxt/prepswinpg.htm; accessed August 17, 2022.

17

Renaissance and Revival

Making something beautiful is difficult, but it is amazingly worthwhile. If you learn to make something in your life truly beautiful—even one thing—then you have established a relationship with beauty. From there you can begin to expand that relationship out into other elements of your life and the world.

—Excerpt from *Beyond Order*
by Jordan B. Peterson

We are entering into something beautiful; I'll even go on to say *glorious*. I believe what we are about to experience in this generation can only be described as Heaven manifesting itself on earth. When the fire came down during the times of Elijah, it was a time to create fear and trembling. I believe that the fire that is falling now will consume us into awe and reverence. A return to holiness through awestruck wonder.

CREATE WILDLY

It is so important to create and to expose ourselves to beauty. As I write, I am on a flight home returning from the English countryside. Parker and I were invited to minister in London, and God moved in power as we led more than 160 people to be baptized, and countless were delivered from demonic spirits. I had always been enthralled with the idea of the English countryside, so we snuck away for two days to retreat and enjoy the beauty.

I have found that in ministry, it is of high importance to stay inspired. I regularly schedule times to put my phone on airplane mode (no service temporarily) so I can be present and create. As I walked the gardens of the countryside, I felt my heart overflowing with gratitude. Taking pause to thank the Lord for all that He had done, to gaze at the flowers and wonder how I could create more spaces of beauty for others to encounter His presence.

Earlier this year, I found myself inspired while scrolling Instagram and finding Jeanne Oliver's account. I felt like her art was communicating things I was experiencing in my spirit. As a "fan girl," I reached out and we quickly became friends (see, social media isn't all bad, ha!). A few weeks later, I invited Jeanne to lead a short creative workshop at our summer Saturate Camp Meeting. The experience was magical as people pushed past comfort and created and painted messy artwork under giant oak trees in North Carolina. As an expert in the creative experience, I have asked Jeanne if she would contribute to the message of this book.

The following is written by my inspiring friend and artist Jeanne Oliver:

How many of us would not accept an inheritance?

I spent many years walking through life with an unclaimed inheritance when it came to my gifts and how I had been creatively made. Whether it was because of words spoken over me, lies I let grow within my own heart, or ideas about how I was supposed to be...I put down the truest parts of who I am.

When I became a mom I started to hear the whispers of the Holy Spirit again, when it came to my creativity. It was a natural unfolding of who I was and who I am; and as I started to connect to that part of myself again, the Lord began to open doors. The Lord was confirming that those parts of how He had made me would get second and third chances to become a reality, even if I had let them pass me by the first time. I was being invited into something more, but I first had to say yes to my gifts. I had to say yes to what was mine.

Many years later, I would drop to my knees in my kitchen and raise my open hands to the Lord. With tears I said, "I give you all of my gifts, anything that is here and I am letting go. I want your plans and not mine." He had already shown Himself to be so faithful and loving with what I was reluctantly and nervously giving Him, that I would have been a fool to not give Him everything.

There were parts of me that I used to think were the mis-fit parts, the quirky parts, the parts that didn't fit in, and the parts so different from other people. Now I know those were (and are) the most beautiful parts of how the Lord has made me. Until I was comfortable setting down the expectations of the world to trust what the Lord had for me, I did not have clear eyes for how I could find the gifts hidden within creativity.

As a child through young adulthood, I believed that serving the Lord looked one way and it did not look like me. I am so thankful to see now that the Lord has allowed me (and you) to MAKE and be invited into intimacy and relationship with the ultimate Maker. To see through living it out that art and making could and would change hearts, lives, and be a connector of beauty for His glory. The Lord uses beauty, art, sculpture, food, gardening, dance, your home, gatherings, and so much more. The Lord uses our gifts given to us first to bring us joy but then to bless others and ultimately to reflect Him. Bust open the boxes of what you thought your creativity could do, crush those old mindsets and run in freedom toward the gifts the Lord has given you. It is literally unlimited what the Lord can do with the beauty you make, see, and share.

One of the greatest weapons of satan is to separate us from making and our creativity. As children we were so connected with it. I knew more of who I truly was when I was a child; the older I got, the more the voices of other adults (and my own) were spoken over me.

Have you ever believed any of these lies?

1. *You are not creative.*

I have been a professional artist and teacher for many years now. When someone hears for the first time that I am an artist, some of the first words I hear uttered from the lips of so many are, "I cannot even draw a stick figure."

Creativity is not just drawing, painting or sculpting. When many hear the word creative, that is what we often can think of. What a funny lie we believe that we are not capable to do something that we might have never tried to do.

The arts is one of the few areas in life that the belief can be, if we can't do it perfectly the first time, then we don't have it in us to do. We never think for a moment it could be because we haven't taken lessons or we haven't practiced. We often believe it is innate or not for us. If I were to hand you a violin and you didn't know how to play you would not think for one second that you are not creative. You would let me know right away that you: 1) have never taken lessons, and 2) have never practiced. You would clearly know and believe that your inability to play the violin was purely based on these two factors. The same is true when it comes to creating. We can believe a lie that we either have it or we don't, and that is not true.

When we believe this lie, we are separating ourselves in a way from discovering more from the Holy Spirit. We are missing the joys of rest, play, being still and present, connecting, and learning as adults to invite imperfect and messy into our journey.

We are missing out on the beauty of being amateurs in something at first and allowing a new skill to grow. Creativity is one of the sweetest gifts given to us from birth, and the older we get the more we forget about it and the blessings that come when we use it.

It's about the invitation to make and create WITH the Creator and the beauty that comes out of that relationship. It can be found in long walks, hands in the garden, cooking for those you love, gathering others for a homecooked meal, transforming a house to a home, the way you listen, the words you write, and yes, even those who put paint to canvas.

2. Creativity is a reward after everything else "important and necessary" is done.

IT'S ABOUT THE INVITATION TO MAKE AND CREATE WITH THE CRE-ATOR AND THE BEAUTY THAT COMES OUT OF THAT RELATIONSHIP.

How often do we all believe this lie! First, I would argue that some of the things we deem important or necessary are actually distractions keeping us from the most beautiful aspects of life, ourselves, beauty, relationships, and even a greater understanding of the Lord.

Being responsible is honoring to the Lord but the truth is that "everything" will not ever be done, which means we put our gifts and creativity down at the bottom when the Lord intended and gave them to us to be at the top.

When we give the best of our day to what we deem necessary, we are giving our leftover time and energy to the beauty the Lord has for us. When we are worn out and tired, when we have stress or anxiety, when we feel separated from others or even the Lord, I believe that so often we are putting aside the one thing that the Lord has given to us that would bring us back (this side of Heaven) to the beauty, connection, intimacy, and rest of the Garden of Eden—creativity.

The Lord is standing with arms overflowing with gifts, abundance, and a different life from what we currently have. Yet, we repeatedly say no. It is often not even a conscious no, but a subconscious no through distractions.

What does stewarding our gifts look like? First it means prioritizing them in our day with all of the other things that we are scheduling as a priority.

When we steward our gifts we are showing through action that we honor the creativity and gifts the Lord has given us. The more we walk out and take hold of our God-given gifts, we'll notice a lot of things on our to do list that don't get done, and it's okay! We will say yes to more of the things the Lord is calling us to do. This shift in perspective changes everything we now deem "necessary."

I have been changed forever because I make. I have had things revealed about me and others, I have been gently walked through forgiveness (of myself and others), I have seen the Lord share His delight in me and I in turn was able to joyfully delight in the Lord. I have become a daily beauty chaser in ways that the younger me would be so proud of.

Calls to Action

I encourage you to find a notepad or use the journal pages at the end of this book and jot these questions down. Then find a place that inspires you and scribble down the answers.

1. Lord, did anyone speak over me or my gifts in a way that has made me question Your gifts as precious and worthy to be pursued and embraced?

2. Lord, have I misinterpreted someone's negative words over my giftings as being about me, when it was really about them and the things they were struggling with? Please help me to be discerning in this area and also forgive others and myself where necessary.

3. Lord, do I have a mindset that has been altered at all about myself, my gifts, creativity, making, and art that believes these parts of myself are a reward after everything "necessary or important" is finished first? Do I believe my gifts get my leftover time and energy instead of the best of me?

4. Is there any place I need to ask Your forgiveness because I didn't see these gifts as good enough, strong enough, powerful enough, beautiful enough? Lord, forgive me for not seeing what You have given me as precious.

5. Lord, thank You for XYZ. Name them! Put them where you will see them every day. Thank the Lord for what He has given you, ask the Lord to reveal any gifts that you are not using and what He would want you to do with them.

6. Does beauty matter to the Lord? If it matters to the Lord then shouldn't it matter to us? Do our lives represent that we serve the God who invites us also into beauty?

7. Schedule time in your day to steward your gifts when you are most alert and energized. You can do laundry, emails, wash dishes, and mow the lawn tired, but you cannot serve your gifts tired.

8. What does a beautiful life look like to you? Do your actions, words, and choices bring you closer or farther away from that beauty?

18

The Seventh Wave— Pioneers and Frontiers

He's not a musician! And you're not a carpenter, and he's not a blacksmith. You are pioneers, and that's all you are until you get there. You have no home, no job, no farm. You have the journey, that's it.

—Dialogue from 1883,
an American Western television drama

There seems to be this strange way that I have noticed the Lord speaking to me lately. God is highlighting certain things that are connected to the direction I am meant to take through the things that grip the attention of my soul. Now, I don't mean things that just seem interesting and worth sharing on social media platforms. I mean things that create what I call a "heart explosion" or better yet, a "burning" within.

After realizing this has become more of a "thing" between the Lord and I, as I have sought His direction and press in for wisdom while leading revival, I began to write down these "heart explosion" moments into a little notebook I keep with my wallet. They can happen at any moment, and I wanted to pay attention to this bread-crumb trail.

Parker tends to be about six months ahead of me prophetically—which is annoying at times!—and he was longing to see the movie *Dune,* the week it came out in theaters. He had read the bestselling book rather quickly, and it would often come up in conversations we would have with other science fiction fans like our favorite waiter at our favorite lunch spot in California.

So when the movie came out, we went to see it during our weekly date night. To be honest, I was pretty apathetic about seeing the movie but wanted to be fair when it came to choosing which movies we see together.

A THEME

I don't know what happened in that theater during those few hours in our reclined leather seats, but I gripped Parker's arm as my soul burned in me. God was speaking to me through sound, colors, and drawing on the agony I feel when thinking of the spirit of evangelism that has been lost within the American church. Betrayal, the doctrine of suffering, imminent war, calling, purpose; all of these themes drew me deeper into discovery like a small child discovering sand at the beach for the first time.

After that moment, I began to notice a theme in the books, movies, shows, heck even in revival history commentaries that began to grip my attention. *Pioneers and new frontiers.* The new thing costs everything. Everywhere I looked, this message was sounding an alarm clock in my spirit.

I believe that God is truly birthing something brand-new in the nations. I think that revival will be expressed quite differently across each nation because each culture has its own ideologies, and precious idols and principalities are different for each nation. I have found it to be somewhat comical and yet utterly heartbreaking to watch ministers create series about the new thing, while doing everything the same old way. The illusion of pioneering with no risk and expecting a reward.

The United States specifically carries a pioneer spirit. The nation was birthed out of radicals seeking religious and political freedoms, willing to risk it all for the mystery of the unknown frontier. The Judeo-Christian values that shaped the ideas behind the American democracy, the Constitution, and culture as a whole were based on the pursuit of life, and well, life more abundantly.

GOD IS TRULY BIRTHING SOMETHING BRAND-NEW.

EUREKA!

Pioneers blazed through rivers, prairies, and mountains searching for gold in the hills. "Eureka!" is what the discoverers yelled as they hammered away and found hidden treasures. My friend, Sher, had studied this subject in-depth, as a California native. "I have found what I am looking for" is what "eureka" means. Is this not the cry of our nation? We are all on a quest for something more. Significance. Meaning. Wealth. Dominion. Order. Freedom. Success.

The gold rush was not for the faint of heart, nor was the pioneer trail to the West. The journey cost everything for most, as they risked everything, sold anything, and adapted to the land and its perils for the sake of a vision of something more.

Is this not the same thing that is happening today? While a divisive culture and slanted news media tries to trap us into its cages of controversy, we can sense a drawing to risk everything for freedom. Freedom of soul, body, and spirit.

We can prove that this longing is true, because of the counterfeits that the enemy is providing so cheaply to a hurting and blind generation. The rise of the New Age movement, social justice movements, and body acceptance posts filling social media feeds are baits. However the reality is, pioneering requires everything. We must count the cost, lay down everything, even what seems good, to discover uncharted territory with the guidance of the Holy Spirit. Paying the cost of everything has its benefits, don't get me wrong. Buying the field where the treasure is will eventually reap a reward.

KEEP GOING!

I think so many of us never enter into the land of promise because the road that leads there is covered in garbage, while the former things are seem to be glittering in gold. "Remember when…" were the words I'd find myself saying in exhaustion to my poor husband as we shared the Gospel in obedience, with no power and no response from the listener. "Remember when we could go on vacation whenever we wanted? Remember when we had full-time salaries while doing ministry? Remember when people made decisions to follow Jesus during our messages?"

The stones of remembrance can as easily become the stones we trip on as we grudgingly finally risk for the small chance that there *may* be gold at the end of the journey. All I can say is, "Keep going!" You don't create family mottos like "Obedience is success" if things work out perfectly all the time! I promise you though, although the journey may feel like it is stripping you of everything you ever held dear, you will reap what you sow in tears, my friend. I am living evidence.

PREPARE A PLACE.

I believe that the seventh wave of revival, which is part of the greatest revival in all of history, is to prepare a place and a people for His glory to come in abundance. Over the last two years, we have seen glimmers of what's available, but I keep hearing the Lord say, "Just wait, you ain't seen nothin' yet."

The truth is, have we created a place where God *can* rule and reign. I know that many people, especially ministers, would respond with an obvious YES! But the reality is, I don't think so. I have seen time and time again, God begin to move in a room and people experience His presence, power, healing, love, and deliverance—and the lead pastor or event organizer shuts down what is happening to "stay on schedule."

We are praying for God to fill our churches with revival, not recognizing they are "our" churches, not His. We have talked the revival talk, but we change nothing. The worst thing the Church can do after the global pandemic of 2020, is to return to "business as usual." Forgive us, Lord, for just postponing our plans, instead of laying them down on the altar to be burned up and asking *You* to resurrect them, if You so desire.

THE BLEEDING EDGE

I believe God is raising up revivalists and apostles who stand on the bleeding edge of the unknown and invite others to take one step farther into mystery for the sake of renaissance. I believe that revivalists are some of the most creative visionaries on the planet. They see, with almost a compulsive obsession, what is not there. They see hope and opportunity in the midst of crisis.

The most broken down, brutalized, wasteland of a city is a sparkling space in the eyes of the revivalist who sees the opportunity to win souls. I am praying for the day when pastors and revivalists can hold hands and skip through wildflowers in perfect unity into the sunset. Yet so often through history, the established traditional church opposes the revivalists' methods, speech, and candor for being too loud, too offensive, and "not church-like enough." We must pioneer, we must provoke, we must take dominion.

Author Dallas Willard writes:

Both human nature and the biblical record suggest to me that the coming government of God, which will displace the power structures of the present world, will not come by any mere progressive advancement of humankind in general. A distinct reentry of the person of Christ, into world history is required, to complete the work. Apart from a radically new principle of life, humanity can simply not advance that far. It is only the real presence of Christ in His mature people interspersed throughout the "secular" life of humanity that will cause the necessary "withering away of the state." The real presence of Christ as a world governing force, will come solely as his called out people occupy their stations in the holiness and power characteristic of him, as they demonstrate to the world the way to live that is best in every respect.[1]

Endnote

1.   Dallas Willard, *The Spirit of the Disciplines: Understanding How God Changes Lives* (New York: HarperOne, 1999).

19

Thirty-Nine Weeks

The Lord spoke to me early June 2022 and said, "America is thirty-nine weeks pregnant with revival."

Luke 7:20-22 (NIV) says:

When the men came to Jesus, they said, "John the Baptist sent us to you to ask, 'Are you the one who is to come, or should we expect someone else?'" At that very time Jesus cured many who had diseases, sicknesses and evil spirits, and gave sight to many who were blind.

This is what happens when Jesus shows up. In the presence of God, there is healing, freedom, and sight restored. Many people talk about "the Presence" like an ethereal concept, unable to recognize that in our services when we refer to the Presence, we are stating that, "the Holy Spirit is here and with Him comes the ways of the Kingdom." We must become so sensitive to the presence and anointing of God and learn to flow with what God is doing in our services, in our families, and throughout our lives.

Luke continues…

> *So he replied to the messengers, "Go back and report to John what you have seen and heard. The blind receive sight, the lame walk, those who have leprosy are cleansed, the deaf hear, the dead are raised, and the good news is proclaimed to the poor. Blessed is anyone who does not stumble on account of me."*
>
> (Luke 7:22-23 NIV)

Jesus replies to their question by motivating messengers. Go back, report what you have seen. Tell people what you have heard. For some of us, we have not yet experienced the supernatural and we haven't seen or heard a thing. So often we are trying to muster up evangelism efforts without an encounter, which leads to burn-out, exhaustion, and becoming apathetic to the whole religious activity. We need to have an experience, and then when we do, we tell people what we have seen or heard.

I believe that we are seeing baptisms sweep our nation and God is raising up consecrated-set apart prophets who are preparing the way of the Lord. If you have been tested, persecuted, attacked, asked to sell all, give all, or have been called to move these last few years—welcome to the remnant. Many of you are called to fields, tents, and the wilderness—and many of you are called to occupy and hold the land and support new apostolic prototypes for a new era of church.

I've noticed while preaching at conferences around the world, during the message, many people may feel burning in their heart, conviction, tingling, fire on their head or on their hands. The Lord is showing up powerfully; and if you're a minister, it's time to throw away your well-rehearsed three-point sermon, get on your hands and knees, and beg the Lord to speak to you and fill you and meet the needs of the people.

*W*HEN THE HOLY SPIRIT DRAWS YOU IN, DO NOT RESIST HIM.

The unfiltered preaching of the Gospel, backed by miracles are a key part of this next move of God. Why? Because this type of preaching requires a response.

John 20:31 (NIV) clearly tells us: *"But these are written that you may believe that Jesus is the Messiah, the Son of God, and that by believing you may have life in his name."* You have something to live for because you have something to die for. You long to be a firebrand of holiness, which is why you'll never be satisfied with status-quo Christianity.

BIRTH PAINS

I believe that since 2016, the United States of America has become pregnant with revival as a nation. One of the primary curses over our country in and out of the Church is the fact that we terminate life and miracles in the womb—in the natural and prophetically—because we can't fully see anything yet. We believe it's the wrong timing, the wrong place, the wrong people, and not our way. Our self-idolatry, control, and fear of the future terminates revival in the land, while it's still in the womb.

God is birthing something at a rapid pace, and it's not in our timing and it's not in our way. America is pregnant with revival and it's already here. The Church is aborting the moves of God because we don't want to allow the painful process of laboring.

We pray for revival; yet the Lord says, "Do you not perceive, do you not see."

Over the past five years, I have given birth three times. I have been pregnant more than not pregnant. With each pregnancy, things really start to change in the third trimester, especially at thirty-nine weeks. I would scoff when friends would say, "I'm so happy for you and Parker, you two are pregnant with another baby!"

No, *we* are not pregnant. We are having a baby, but *I* am pregnant.

When pregnant, everything is affected by what God is creating and birthing in you. I believe that millions around the world are going to experience the joys of revival, but I believe that there is a remnant who will become pregnant with it. They will birth the move of God through prayer, sacrifice, and radical obedience.

When you are pregnant, you are always conscious of what you are carrying. You can't eat what you want you, you can't sleep when you want, pregnancy requires your full attention. When carrying my babies in my womb, it was fascinating when I felt the baby moving. No one can convince a pregnant woman that she is not pregnant, because she feels *the movement of life* inside her.

Can you feel what God's doing in this nation?

Our prayers need to switch from, "Lord, Lord, bring revival!" To "Lord, Lord, I am ready. I am on my front foot. I'm packing up my hospital bags, and I'm waiting on my front foot, I'm ready!"

Labor begins when the water breaks. Do you see the baptism waters saturating the beaches, the church parking lots, the streets, and in tents? You better move when the water breaks! You have to get rid of the distractions, focus, prepare, and engage.

I encourage you, dear reader, *stay on your assignment* and don't be distracted. America is thirty-nine weeks pregnant! Don't change the subject, *keep going!* Don't get tired of the "revival conversations" keep pressing in.

OUR PRAYERS NEED TO SWITCH FROM, "LORD, LORD, BRING REVIVAL!" TO "LORD, LORD, I AM READY."

Although it may be the early stages, let's not terminate the birth before it even begins to take form. God's been trying to wake us, shake us, and show us that the things we are earnestly desiring are outside the four walls of the churches.

> *So resist the temptation to pronounce premature judgment on anything before the appointed time when all will be fully revealed. Instead, wait until the Lord makes his appearance, for he will bring all that is hidden in darkness to light and unveil every secret motive of everyone's heart. Then, when the whole truth is known, each will receive praise from God.*
>
> (1 Corinthians 4:5 The Passion Translation)

In these last days, there will be many very *real* miracles, revival outbreaks, and moves of God. And for every real move, there will be five counterfeits. Do not lose hope. Stay in the Word, get into His presence, and surround yourself with others who are living the life that bears with the fruit of repentance.

Parker says, "Jessi, relax, the fruit always bears out." What does that mean? Thorns and thistles can't produce grapes.

If you're anything like me, you can feel angst at the number of false teachers and preachers parading about. I have run out of too many green rooms and conferences hysterically crying after encountering counterfeiters. But despite all that, I still believe and hope in the best. I have met several prophets who are the real deal, and their words cut right to the heart with revelation and the breath of God.

God is orchestrating events for His glory during this moment in history. Our job in this hour is simply to pray and respond to whatever we hear the Lord saying.

*L*IVE LIKE SLAVES TO RIGHTEOUSNESS, UNTANGLED FROM SIN.

The signs of the Third Great Awakening are here. Saints are being equipped and sent out in power—the sick are healed, demons are being cast out, and social media feeds are flooded with repentance and spontaneous baptisms!

We need to live like slaves to righteousness, untangled from sin.

What shall we say, then? Shall we go on sinning so that grace may increase? By no means! We are those who have died to sin; how can we live in it any longer? Or don't you know that all of us who were baptized into Christ Jesus were baptized into his death? We were therefore buried with him through baptism into death in order that, just as **Christ was raised from the dead through the glory of the Father, we too may live a new life.** *For if we have been united with him in a death like his, we will certainly also be united with him in a resurrection like his. For we know that* **our old self was crucified with him** *so that the body ruled by sin might be done away with, that* **we should no longer be slaves to sin**—*because anyone who has died has been set free from sin.*

(Romans 6:1-7 NIV)

— 185 —

I encourage you to decide today to finally die to that old life and receive the new life you say you want. Set yourself apart for revival and be baptized and filled with the Holy Spirit.

> The next day John saw Jesus coming toward him and said, "Look, the Lamb of God, who takes away the sin of the world! This is the one I meant when I said, 'A man who comes after me has surpassed me because he was before me.' I myself did not know him, but the reason I came baptizing with water was that he might be revealed to Israel." Then John gave this testimony: "I saw the Spirit come down from heaven as a dove and remain on him. And I myself did not know him, but the one who sent me to baptize with water told me, 'The man on whom you see the Spirit come down and remain is the one who will baptize with the Holy Spirit.' **I have seen and I testify that this is God's Chosen One."**
>
> (John 1:29-34 NIV)

If not now, then when? America shall be saved.

Journal

As you read, jot down any ideas, visions or things the Holy Spirit is highlighting to you.

_____

_____

_____

_____

_____

_____

_____

_____

_____

_____

_____

_____

_____

_____

_____

_____

SATURATE

SATURATE

SATURATE

SATURATE

SATURATE

SATURATE

JOURNAL

SATURATE

About Jessi Green

Jessi was born and raised on Long Island, New York. In 2007 she moved to Manhattan and worked in the nightclub industry as a doorman and nightclub promoter. In 2009, she was radically saved in her apartment after a traumatic breakup and drug-filled lifestyle.

After encountering the love and power of the real living Jesus, she sold her belongings and traveled to fifteen countries over eleven months, working with orphanages, preaching the Gospel, praying for the sick, and sharing the love of Jesus.

She then moved back to Manhattan and started a successful social media agency working with luxury brands worldwide. In 2012, she met her husband, Parker Green, and stepped into full-time ministry. In 2016, the Greens moved to Southern California and founded Salt Churches. Everything in the Greens' lives changed after thousands were saved, healed, and baptized on the beaches of California in 2020, launching Saturate Global.

Jessi is a revivalist, preacher, wife, mom, visionary, and creative type. Along with raising their three children—David Leonidas, Ethan

Everest, and Summer Kingsley—she is the director of Saturate Global, a grassroots revival movement uniting the Church by reaching those who don't know Jesus, baptizing them, and making disciples who multiply.

She believes that everyone is qualified to preach the Gospel and teach others to follow Jesus. While enjoying the sun in North Carolina, she passionately speaks about what it means to follow Jesus who is *alive* and wants to transform cities and your personal life. Her first book, *Wildfires*, will ignite you to have a burning passion for Jesus and be a catalyst of revival.

YOU CAN FOLLOW JESSI ON

INSTAGRAM

 https://instagram.com/jessi.green

ONLINE

 JessiGreen.com.

From

Jessi Green

Where is the Jesus I *thought* I was following?

If your faith feels more like a dying ember than a radiant light, perhaps you haven't met the real Jesus.

At her core, Jessi felt dry and lifeless. Weary of anemic religion, she had almost given up on Christianity, until one day, she came face to face with the real Jesus whose eyes burn like fire! His gaze lit a spark within her, fanning the tinder of her soul into a glowing blaze.

Today, Jessi burns with a vision to see a holy fire sweep across the nation. She and her husband, Parker, lead the Saturate OC revival movement in California, where they introduce thousands of people to the real Jesus, and see lives radically changed!

You are just a few pages away from a similar encounter. In *Wildfires,* Jessi Green invites you to let Jesus breathe upon the embers of your soul, until your whole life burns for Him!

This is the moment where you break free from feeble religion and a decaying culture. Lay your life upon the altar, and let Jesus kindle a wildfire in you!

Purchase your copy wherever books are sold.

Other Spirit-Filled Books On Revival

Open Heavens
Bill Johnson

Reformers Arise
Cindy Jacobs

Digging the Wells of Revival
Lou Engle

True Stories of the Miracles of Azusa Street and Beyond
Tommy Welchel

Doorkeepers of Revival
Kim Owens

Reclaiming Revival
Corey Russell

When the Heavens are Brass
John Kilpatrick

The River of Zion
Tommy Welchel with Jody Keck

RevivalMakers
Tony Suarez

Rivers of Revival
Elmer L. Towns

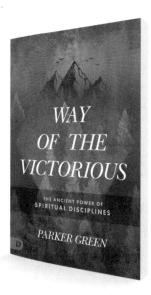

Saturate Global

Saturate is a grassroots revival movement in America.

We exist to create a space for people to experience the tangible presence of God and the fullness of His love and power.

Sign up for more information and events at
SaturateGlobal.com